RETHINK
EVERYTHING

RETHINK
Everything

THE COURAGE TO LEAD DIFFERENTLY

KRISTI H. TURNER

Kaizen Consulting, Inc.

Rethink Everything

Published by Kaizen Consulting, Inc.

Book Design: Dino Marino, www.dinomarino.com

Paperback ISBN: 979-8-9866502-0-3

Hardcover ISBN: 979-8-9866502-2-7

eBook ISBN: 979-8-9866502-1-0

"Turner speaks to the importance of listening and caring for employees, customers, and ourselves as key elements of leadership. Her lessons and insights are strong examples of what I call, Caring Leadership™, taking daily actions in ways that show concern and kindness to those we lead."

— **Heather R Younger**, *CEO of Employee Fanatix, Two-Time TEDx Speaker, Bestselling Author of The Art of Caring Leadership*

"This is my kind of leadership book — one that celebrates a truly integrated life, thoughtfully challenges the status quo, and normalizes the conversation around intentional rest. I'm confident that Turner's journey, and the priceless insights she shares, will inspire more leaders to rebel for the change they want to see in their lives, companies, and the world."

— **Shelley Paxton**, *Chief Soul Officer, Rebel Leader, and Bestselling Author of Soulbbatical*

"Powerful advice for business managers and leaders from one of the strongest executives and top marketers I've ever had the privilege of working with. Turner shows us the importance of authenticity, diversity, and accountability at the top, and shares actionable insights on making better decisions in both business and our personal lives."

— **Campbell B. Lanier, III**, *Chairman & CEO of ITC Holdings, Serial Technology Entrepreneur, and Investor*

"This book shows us the power of trusting your gut, creating your own path, and refusing to compromise your values along the way. A great read for anyone who wants to blaze new trails while maintaining healthy relationships and boundaries in their personal and professional life."

— **Laura Anton**, *Former VP Visa Marketing Consulting*

"In a world where most are forced to make a choice between living in their head or their heart, Turner chose to lead with both. And in these pages, she shows us how to do the same. An inspiring and potentially career-advancing read."

— **Paul Dodd**, *Chief Revenue Officer,*
Enigma Technologies, Inc

"*Rethink Everything* is like having a mentor at your fingertips. Turner provides practical insights from her years of experience navigating the complexities of corporate life from a human perspective - as a wife, mother, friend, and a very driven and successful business leader. She shows us that success is not a straight line but keeping your personal values and integrity at the forefront will get you exactly where you want to be, in this season and the next."

— **Laura Wilbanks**, *Former Global Chief Marketing Officer,*
Thomson Reuters

"Contemplative insights on trusting your intuition and finding fulfillment in life and business. It's one thing to want to trust yourself and another to actually embody that trust. In *Rethink Everything*, Turner shows us how."

— **Dori Salisbury**, *SVP of Operations, Searchspring*

"*Rethink Everything* encourages us to lead with integrity and show up as our whole selves. With poignant examples and candid reflections, Turner shows us how authenticity and accountability are essential for making our teams and companies even more successful, and how using the corporate platforms we are privileged to have can be used to do good for all."

— **Alisa Arner**, *Vice President of Consumer Sales for The Americas, Microsoft*

"A triumph on becoming the best version of yourself! Turner provides a poignant and powerful reminder of the lessons we learn through the journey of life, and how to apply them with purpose and passion. With its thoughtful storytelling and practical advice, *Rethink Everything* will both challenge and encourage you in ways that will have lasting impact, personally and professionally."

— **Craig Wood**, *CEO Premier International*

"A must-read for every business leader, manager, and working parent…Turner reminds us leadership starts from the heart, being human, having compassion, and redefining processes for the better, instead of simply accepting the status quo.

— **Carmen Barreto-Cruz**, *SVP Americas, InComm*

"A rare leadership book that is practical, accessible, and emphasizes the humanity of diverse thinking. Turner shares countless examples of leading with good-faith collaboration, creativity, honesty, humility, and humor."

— **Heather Heebner**, *VP of Human Resources, Instant Financial*

"*Rethink Everything* is a must-read book on leadership, business, family and life balance. Such an insightful journey with practical tips to help you get to know yourself and improve all aspects of your life. Turner's entertaining stories bring key leadership characteristics to the surface such as being determined, hard-working and possessing grit. She also shows the more subtle leadership skills that often get overlooked such as being empathetic, respectful, humble, and trusting your gut. Unlike most leadership books, this is shared from a very human perspective: it will make you laugh, it will make you cry, and it might even make you *Rethink Everything*."

— **Suzanne Beisner**, *Managing Partner, Customer Focused Strategies*

DEDICATION

To my husband, Wes and my two amazing kids,
Lexie and Jack for all your love and support.
You have made me a better leader and a better human.

To my extended family, friends, and career bosses,
coworkers, mentors, and team members.
You made a difference in my life,
and I am forever grateful.

CONTENTS

SEASON THREE:
THE LEADERSHIP YEARS: VIEW FROM THE TOP, TEAM DYNAMICS, AND RAISING THE NEXT GENERATION

RETHINKING THE HUSTLE:
A GLOBAL PANDEMIC, SOULBBATICAL, AND GETTING COMFORTABLE WITH THE UNCOMFORTABLE

ABOUT THE BOOK

*One corporate leader's climb to the top
while refusing to sacrifice family for career
and finding her power to lead differently.*

In *Rethink Everything* we walk with Kristi Turner in each season
of her career journey through corporate management, as she
shares poignant *notes to self*, illustrating how they influenced her
life decisions. As Turner shows, from the slightest whisper to the
most dramatic experiences, life's micro moments' drive our soft-
and hard-coded belief systems, which in turn inform every choice
we make in life and define how we lead ourselves and others.

Turner weaves together stories of challenges, observations,
and lessons learned from her childhood, ballet days, marriage,
parenting, and career, to finding herself as the only woman in the
corporate boardroom. She offers a fresh lens on pay inequality and
the power of diversity. The reader sees how she fits in while still
staying authentic to herself and her innate desire to work hard,
be thoughtful, take risks, and make a difference. She illustrates
the power of pausing, trusting your intuition, and mustering the
courage to challenge the status quo, when the status quo just
doesn't make sense. By sharing this honest portrayal of what
it means to lead herself while consciously being aware of her
sphere of influence—those she interacts with both professionally

and personally—she opens our eyes to the value of awareness, authenticity, and accountability.

With wisdom, generosity, and grace Kristi Turner illustrates how our personal and professional lives can each enhance rather than be detrimental to each other. This idea that we should all pause and rethink everything periodically to check in is a priceless lesson that can benefit every individual, manager, leader, and business.

NOTE TO READER

This past year, I took a break from my busy life as Chief Marketing Officer of a technology company. I was in my 50s and I had been working since I was 14 years old. It felt like a good time to reflect before I decided on my next chapter. I needed a change of atmosphere and a different challenge. I simply wanted to pause the hustle for a reevaluation period. In the process, I learned a lot about myself and all the *notes to self* that were behind my career decisions and my management style.

This book was beginning to develop in my head. Publishing a book had always been a bucket list item, so why not now? Many thought I was crazy. Why put yourself out there? Why be vulnerable? I understood that it may have looked like a midlife crisis, but it wasn't that at all. It was more of a midlife deeper awakening. It was more about documenting what I learned on my journey for those that were in the middle of their own journey, things I wish someone had told my younger self, so I didn't have to figure them out on my own.

One of my dear friends, a co-executive, met me for lunch a few weeks after my resignation. She asked me the obvious question, "Okay, I'm dying to know. How are you feeling away from the chaos, no emergency texts, no meetings, what's it like?"

I thought for a moment and replied, "It feels like skydiving. That is the best analogy I can give you. I just jumped out of the corporate plane, and I feel like I am free falling from a high altitude, and it's scary. I mean the adrenaline is going with pure excitement but also with fear. I'm free falling and looking back toward the plane, and it just keeps going. It's like it didn't even slow down when I jumped out. Some of the people in the plane that I thought would stay in touch, didn't. Some people that I thought would at least be looking down wishing me luck aren't even looking.

So, I'm free falling my friend, but somehow, I know it was the right decision, and I have peace about it. I don't know how I know, but I know. After I fall a few thousand feet, I'm going to stop looking back at the plane and to where I've been, and I'm going to pull the cord. There is going to be an abrupt jerk that skyrockets me upward, like a wake-up call. Then, I'm going to look up and see the most colorful parachute ever. And I'm going to turn my gaze forward. The view, oh the view, is going to be spectacular. It's a view that I would have never seen if I hadn't jumped out of that plane. It's quiet and peaceful and lonely, but in a good way. It's like I finally have enough silence and time to take it all in and start steering the parachute in the direction I want to go. I don't quite know exactly where I am going to land. I have to trust the wind, the sky, the parachute...I am 5000 feet in the air going on faith. Right now, the free fall is scary as hell."

Now with the benefit of hindsight, my analogy was right, that is exactly what happened. I see the whole world from a completely different perspective than I did before. It was one of the riskiest decisions I had ever made financially, but it was the best decision I ever made. I was taking a *Soulbbatical*, credit to author and friend Shelley Paxton. It wasn't all sunshine and rainbows, quite the opposite. When you slow down for the first time in your life, there are a lot of feelings and emotions that come up. This book started out as a book on business leadership, yet it transformed along the way into a book about how I got to where I am and all the micro choices I made and notes to self I had along the way. We all have them.

When I paused, I realized so much of our business and personal life is in a reactive, almost defensive mode as the world seems to come at us unannounced. It hits us with challenges, opportunities, devastations, and a lot of "shouldas." Sometimes, we need to allow ourselves some quiet, alone time to soak up the wisdom we have acquired along the way. Sometimes, we don't even realize the influences that are planting deep belief systems into our being.

We are randomly born in a particular geographic place into a particular family or to no family. Depending on our birth lotto, our surroundings, and our upbringing, it can be nurturing and positive or it can be challenging and horrific. As we experience things in life at every age, we consciously and unconsciously continue to adopt belief systems and develop coping mechanisms. There can be significant moments that obviously impact us but there are also tiny moments that on the surface seem insignificant, yet in hindsight we realize drove many of our life decisions, relationships, and our personality styles.

If we don't pause occasionally, and look back to see what is true, what is exaggerated, and what is limiting, we might miss the opportunity to redefine what is right for us. The big beliefs and the small beliefs drive our daily decisions, worry lists, and leadership style.

Things were so black and white or good and bad when I was younger and now things are grayer, as I have a better understanding of why I am who I am and why I do what I do. More importantly I have more empathy for others. We are all imperfect humans leading ourselves and those around us. Is there a better way to lead? It feels like there is a change in our midst. A season for us all to lead ourselves better, to be a force of good within our sphere of influence and challenge some things that are serving a few.

By giving myself permission to rethink everything— my leadership style, career ambitions, health, relationships, spirituality, investments, and belief system—I consciously let go of what felt inauthentic and no longer served me. This same process strengthened my beliefs and relationships in ways that resonated with my soul. What I learned was that how I lead myself impacts how I lead others. Spoiler alert: it's all intermingled and that is exactly how it should be.

My hope is that *Rethink Everything* gives you the courage to do the same, as we are all leaders, regardless of what we do or where we are at in our lives. You are the leader of your life and influential to many around you. Take the time to understand your own notes to self. Empower yourself to challenge the status quo and listen to that voice inside you. It changes everything.

To my readers, you will find this book different than most leadership books. This was by design, as I find most leadership books boring, textbook-like, and extremely difficult to get through. I wanted this book to be relatable, reflect reality, and be an easy read. I believe we learn more through storytelling than other methods. This book is filled with stories.

It opens with a scene from the boardroom that is a day I would rather forget, but drove me to question how I got there and reflect on who I am. To answer those questions, I chose to reflect back to each season in my life to discover what drove my "whys" and created my leadership style. The book is divided into four sections: Season 1: The Early Years, Season 2: Working Mom Life, Season 3: The Leadership Years and last section Rethinking the Hustle.

You will find *Season 1: The Early Years* includes a look back on key events in my childhood that impacted my young adulthood from love, laughter, and family to murder, divorce, and death. As a reader, I think you will find relatable moments when you think of your own childhood. We all have family dynamics, geographical cultures, teachers, and coaches that formulate our beliefs and values at a young age, before we have the consciousness to form our own. It is also where I formulated my work ethic from a decade as a classical ballet dancer. For you, it might have been sports, band, or a first job. Each of us has different types of first experiences that lay the foundation for how we see the world and pursue meaning in life. Reflecting in hindsight gives us a greater understanding of our decisions and why we are who we are.

Season 2: Working Mom Life focuses on the critical years in middle management, marriage, and the decision to have kids. You will see the influence of early bosses and mentors, the power of trusting your gut and challenging the old way of doing things in business. You will find real work and life, employee and management experiences that just might give you a different perspective on how you see your own work opportunities and the rules of the game. What I hope you will see even more is how my decision to have children and work, not only enhanced my joy in life, but made me a better manager and a more attuned mother.

In *Season 3: The Leadership Years*, the focus is more on what it felt like reaching the top and being the only female in the boardroom. You will find insights on the board and executive team dynamics that can elevate or derail a company. You will get a unique perspective of pay inequality and diversity that may surprise you. You will learn how to create a strong camaraderie among your team as a manager and key decision-making techniques for when you are under stress. It is packed full of tips on creating better employee cultures and what employees crave at work. Most importantly, you will get proven tactical stress-reducing tools that we all need in business and in life.

Lastly, in *Rethinking the Hustle*, although it covers a much shorter period in time, this section shows the reality of the "busyness addiction" so many of us adopt in our lives, and the power of pausing and giving yourself a little grace to catch your breath. It is not about leaving your job—it is about redefining for yourself what you really want and what you don't want. It's about giving ourselves permission to explore, rest a little more, and be a little kinder to ourselves.

This book is for today's managers and executives who are always seeking to be better, want to drive bottom-line results, elevate their team's collaboration, and create more positive employee cultures for themselves and those around them. This book is also for anyone who wants to create a more intentional alignment between their values and their lived experiences, in career, family, relationships, and life.

Consider this book permission to pause, trust your intuition, and *Rethink Everything*.

Kristi H. Turner

January 2023

THE BOARDROOM—
WHERE IT HAPPENED

I knew what was going to happen. The players were all in the room. I had been at a tradeshow in a different city and asked to fly in for an emergency executive meeting. I had felt it coming for weeks, but this was the heated moment I had been dreading. Many lives were about to change. As one of only two women on the executive team, it felt both empowering and unfair at the same time. Even though I had made it to the top and was at the table as one of the decision-makers, I didn't have a vote. Yet I was going to have to deal with the consequences. It was going to be a shitshow.

Four of the twelve people in the room had a new plan. They'd had a pre-meeting. I read the body language. The frequent eye contact between them was obvious. They had orchestrated who would say what, and how to make it look spontaneous. It felt like a planned execution, well-thought-out, and crafted with intention. Was I the only one seeing it? Had everyone sensed it was coming? Was I reading the room wrong? I would never know for sure. The political positioning and private one-on-one conversations had been epic over the preceding few weeks. There were two different layoff plans in play. Each had an opposing list of affected executives. The surprise was that two executives were playing both sides. The pain of the betrayal was deep, as I had respected and trusted them until that moment. I thought they were "good" guys, making this betrayal hit more deeply.

The shift of power began. The tension in the room was a result of our CEO being fired by our board. Our executive team of twelve was a ridiculously large number, but a series of acquisitions had created a need to give everyone a position. There were the original entrepreneurs, one investor's chosen execs, and the venture capital firm's chosen execs, all thrown together with their incongruent and competing backgrounds and experiences.

The year prior had been the most stressful environment I'd worked in during my 25-year career. We had all experienced a little ego power-driven leadership common in corporate cultures, but this was at an inconceivable level. Years earlier a business mentor of mine had recommended a book on sociopaths in leadership. Before reading it, I believed even the toughest bosses still cared for the basic humanness of those they managed. I was wrong. I'm not a psychiatrist, but what I was witnessing checked every box according to the book. This was self-protection at all costs. The outcome of their plan meant laying off over a hundred unsuspecting employees. It was disgusting to witness, and no longer confined to the pages of a book about sociopaths. Was I in a movie? These things didn't happen in real life. Or did they? Could people truly be this malevolent?

My insides were on fire. I could barely distinguish between the past, present, and future, as scenes from all were hitting me simultaneously. How did we get here? What went wrong? Scenes from my memory converged. The former CEO uttering curse words at me for twenty minutes, demanding more, while constantly changing the metrics for success. I'd been doing exactly what he'd asked me to. I couldn't comprehend how his brain, heart, and soul worked. Dealing with him caused me to think back to a point made in the book my mentor had given me: sociopaths do not have the ability to empathize. They are 100% self-centered. They also have an ability to convince themselves that they are good and honest. They believe they are doing good. So maybe he felt nothing.

Although no longer present, the former CEO had used fear-based management to drive results, pitting one executive against another. He repetitively raised the goals and key performance indicators to ensure they were unachievable, thereby giving himself leverage to fire anyone at any time. Every executive responded differently. For me, it was sleepless nights. Breakfast was impossible. I threw up at least once a day. Another executive was popping Tums like candy and had heart palpitations when he laid down to sleep. Another's marriage was falling apart, and another had severe back pain. Still another made jokes and was seemingly unimpacted, but later I learned had a negative talk track going on in his head that would make the most confident leader fold into the fetal position. This didn't feel right. A job, even a top leadership job, brings with it expected stress and difficult decisions, but it shouldn't erode your health or encroach on your personal life. This, at every level of my conception, was wrong. It was just wrong.

Back to the room where it happened: with twelve executives and one board member sitting around a large conference room, the dance was on. The first of the four in cahoots started with the classic position, "I wouldn't want the CEO position if you paid me a million dollars, but I am just going to throw it out there if it means saving this company, I will do whatever you all want me to do." (Sociopath code for I want the CEO position.)

Second of the four, the charismatic one, whose opinion changed with the wind, chimed in on script, "Well now that you bring it up, that is something we should consider." The third one said, "We need to look at all options, and that is one we should consider." The fourth offered his support.

Let the games begin.

They casually presented a Plan B as if it was a freshly conceived product of on-the-spot brainstorming. They thought they were pulling it off, not giving away the staging and scripting, but the rest of us could smell the bullshit.

Over the next hour, tensions rose. One of my dear executive friends at the table, who was still thinking we were on Plan A before the surprise Plan B showed up, lost it on all of them. The f-bomb was thrown back and forth as if it was the most common word in the English language. The board member present tried to douse the flames. I sat between the f-bomb executive and one of the four traitors, who had his back to me, and said nothing. I could feel the sting of my eyes wanting to well up but wouldn't deign to let that happen. I knew how to stop tears. I blinked repetitively and a soft blow upward from the bottom lip. It worked most of the time. I was a woman, and refused to be labeled as too emotional, or too empathetic toward employees if I dared let a tear show. I had practice. Isn't a male executive literally losing it, yelling, and cussing like a street thug being too emotional? Oh no. For a man it is considered powerful, passionate, and tough, not emotional.

I caught the eye of the other female executive for two seconds. We knew. It is amazing what a look could do across the room. It was like she said, "I know, and I understand, but don't you dare cry. Don't give them the satisfaction. Hold it together." I did.

Then, I spoke up. I had preached about the importance of speaking up to innumerable younger females climbing the corporate ladder and now I had to say something. Funny, I don't remember what I uttered exactly, but it was something about a logical compromise option that was somewhere in between Plan A and Plan B. They were just words, I knew this as I said them, and everyone in the room knew when they heard them. By this time, my vote didn't matter. The moves were in play. It was over, and they were going to execute Plan B regardless of what was said.

And just like that, over the next couple of weeks, the paths of hundreds of people's lives were diverted. Their paychecks stopped. They were jobless, not because they had done a bad job.

Their skill sets, talents, performances, and potential weren't even considered. Some people were put on the list just because the new CEO knew they didn't agree with him.

Where was the fairness? Where was karma? Was this even legal? Could one mentally unstable person just put an innocent employee on a list and fire them for no reason? Yes, they could. Yes, it was legal. The root cause of this entire situation was two bad hires. The board had hired the first CEO who had overspent, putting the company into financial jeopardy. Then the board hired the second CEO, who made some of the most illogical decisions I had ever seen. Repeat mistake one with mistake two.

Fast forward five years and enter the irony of karma and time. The second CEO was fired for unethical behavior. The chair of the board served jail time for an unethical and illegal act in his personal life. Surprised? Not at all.

Something had to change. It was time to rethink everything—being a leader, being a parent, being healthy, relationships, the universe, and my belief system.

Who am I?

WHO AM I?

I am a successful American businesswoman by societal definitions. I have held several SVP Marketing and Chief Marketing Officer (CMO) positions in various multimillion-dollar technology companies. Most recently, I was the only female at the C-level, the highest level other than the board room in the corporate hierarchy. I had "made it" by all accounts. I had climbed the corporate ladder and was well respected. I was at the table.

I was married to a good man, the mother of two amazing children, the aunt to fourteen remarkable nieces and nephews. One of four siblings who adored their mother. My personal life was full despite the common negative portrayal society and Hollywood puts on working moms. Some facets of our society want everyone to think a working mom is stressed out, on the verge of a breakdown, and unable to be a good parent. There was a lot on my plate. I was tired, but I was present. I was fully present for my children and for my job. I am not sure how, when I consider it today, but I had prioritized my kids from the day they were born, and I hardly missed a moment of their lives. My son and daughter were aware of my work, but knew I was available. I even missed a board meeting once because my son had an event at his grade school. I remember a co-executive saying it was a career death sentence to miss a board meeting. So be it.

There was one thing I would neither compromise nor negotiate, and that was my kids. Family was my priority.

There were so many other life lessons that I still hadn't quite grasped. The corporate politics, unfairness, and even unethical behavior was still haunting me. I believe everything that comes up in our lives offers some type of a life lesson. I knew it was critical for me to learn from it. I wasn't quite sure what the lesson was. What I did know was if I didn't figure it out now, it would just come up again until I did. Learn it now or learn it later. My choice.

I had observed women and men before me reach the C-suite. Each one approached it differently and made unique life choices. My career started in the early 1990s when sexual harassment was the norm and reporting its occurrence meant the female was fired and rendered unhirable by another company in the future. The man initiating the sexual harassment was either paid well to leave with a recommendation or told to tone it down and stay exactly where he was with zero consequences. Let's just say sometimes the consequences don't fit the crime. It wasn't right, but it was reality then.

The presence of women at the top, while limited, inspired me to forge my own path. Most, not all, of the executive women I met had chosen not to have children. Most of the men I witnessed at the top had a stay-at-home spouse, or at a minimum, fewer "home" responsibilities. They had more freedom to focus on their job and travel at a moment's notice. It seemed to be so much easier for them. As soon as I found someone in an executive role with children, and a life that looked close to what I had envisioned for myself, they changed. They chose to leave the corporate world, work as a consultant or divorce. My only option was to be inspired by the bits and pieces from different mentors that fit me and ignore the rest. I didn't want to divorce. I wanted to be home and present for myself, my husband, and my kids. I wasn't willing to be an asshole boss or betray coworkers in a political battle. I wanted to be me. It felt like it was going to be a lonely journey.

So, along the rise up the corporate ladder, I figured it out on my own. I realized that most leaders were male, and the corporate system had been created by them for them. I took on many male leadership styles to advance in corporate America. It was the only strategy I saw at the time. It was a challenge. Imitating the masculine traits of the corporate world were in stark contrast to my years as a ballerina where femininity dominated. Being an observer and tapping into my intuition were my superpowers. I observed, learned, and quickly figured out what I needed to lean toward to make the room full of men comfortable with my presence. I was able to be there, adopting several masculine leadership traits while taking advantage of being the only woman in the room. My female self stood out just by being present. It was an advantage as much as it was a disadvantage. The irony. My career was a privilege. I had broken the glass ceiling, but it didn't feel like I had quite arrived.

I had learned to pivot and morph with the best of them. I studied up on the language used by the ones that were praised and promoted. I watched as they figured it out, how they behaved and made decisions. They focused on the big boulders and didn't sweat the small stuff. They traced their decisions to bottom line impact. They made bold moves that got them noticed. I didn't question much in the early years. I just kept learning and adopting. Many assumed I had been working toward a CMO position for my whole life, but nothing could have been further from the truth. I simply had an ambition to be really good at whatever I was doing, and I had a competitive mindset. In other words, if I saw someone really good, I wanted to be a little bit better than them. Every time I "conquered" one job I saw another one I wanted. It was one job at a time.

Early on in my career, I was a classic overachiever, producing at lightning speed. I had grit and a work ethic that outpaced most. I was direct, blunt and had little patience for underachievers and absolutely loathed what I perceived as incompetence. Several of my early bosses had coached me on being more patient with others, but I didn't quite see the need. There was so much to get done! In my 20s my response was simple, "If they aren't producing, why should I encourage them?" I didn't understand why underachievers or underperformers were kept in their jobs. Let's just hire the best and keep the best, was my thinking. Why are we accepting mediocrity? Why would any company or organization want mediocrity? It didn't make sense to me.

My life track consisted of a series of predictable overachieving milestones. I was in the top 2% of almost everything I did, but never quite top dog. This was perfectly fine with me. I might not have been the smartest, the best looking, or the most talented in the room but I had grit. At some point in my 20s, I read a study on primates that, looking back, must have planted a seed in my subconscious. The study measured the stress level of an entire pack of primates. It basically found that the most stressed individuals in the troop were the highest-ranking alphas and the lowest ranking. Most, if not all, animal species have a pecking order, even humans. In every community, the study repetitively found that the leader, the alpha, male or female, had the highest stress equal only to those lowest in the social hierarchy. It made perfect sense to me at the time. If you had no money, no status, and no influence, you were highly stressed. You had no control. You were fed last. If you were the one in charge of all decisions and overall health of the community, you had all the pressure, and as a result were also highly stressed. The ones in between had less stress. I was an overachiever, but I was also smart. I decided early on I wanted to be wildly successful but not number one. Somewhere in my brain I had determined that would be the best of all worlds. I wasn't wrong.

I chose to be the number one's best friend and greatest supporter. In my ballet days, I was the understudy for the prima ballerina. I had the fairy godmother role in Cinderella and was Cinderella's understudy. I was her best friend, supporting her in the very demanding role of being the best. I was Chief Marketing Officer, CMO to the Chief Executive Officer, CEO. My job was literally to make the CEO look good. Being CEO is a lonely position, every top dog needs someone they can trust to talk things out. In different jobs, the description might have been customer service, operations, or marketing, but in some roles, not all, my greatest responsibility was being a supportive confidante, friend, and encourager to number one. I loved it.

I never fit well into the predefined society boxes, literally and figuratively. Every survey asked if I was white, Hispanic, Black, Indian, or Asian. I was white, Cuban, and Belgian. What box should I check? You could only check one. I was a unique combination that gave me something special, but it also made me feel different. I was a unicorn. I was an extrovert *and* an introvert. I was a dark-skinned tomboy ballerina with boobs next to the preferred light-skinned, flat-chested dancers. I was a middle child that carried traits of an oldest child. I had strong female energy but carried many traits typically associated with males. I felt wealthy and poor at the same time. I didn't fit into the Democratic or the Republican box as I was equally passionate about building profitable businesses, minimizing taxes, being accountable for my own life, lending a helping hand and saving the earth. I was financially conservative, yet the first to lend a helping hand to those who needed a lift. I had equally active left brain and right brain thought patterns. I was analytical *and* creative.

As a marketing executive, I would dive into the data and spreadsheets one day and then write the outline of a creative video script the next. This dichotomy of talents was both a blessing and a curse because it was difficult to choose directions and areas on which to focus throughout my life. I loved so many things simultaneously. I loved ballet, gymnastics, swimming, and skiing. I loved business. I loved to write. I loved being a parent and my family. I loved horses. I loved being with friends and being alone. I loved managing people. I loved. Sometimes I just loved too much, yet I wasn't great at receiving love.

Life had been good to me. I enjoyed interacting with so many different types of individuals. I learned something from each of them and I prayed I had contributed to them in a positive way. I didn't shy away from honest feedback and over time I learned how to receive criticism and grow. I always gave more than I received. That was my comfort zone. I didn't like owing anyone anything. It didn't matter if it was a favor or money. Debt was not something I participated in—ever. Yes, like so many others, I never asked for help, a trait I would later learn was not something to be proud of, and incredibly detrimental to my overall well-being.

With full awareness and intent, I had surrounded myself with amazing people. I had my pack. Each was different in their own way but served a purpose in my life. There was my family, both immediate and extended, that was a mutual exchange of love and support.

Outside of family, I had strong business, spiritual and wellness mentors. I had a strong group of amazing girlfriends, that were my tight-knit group of confidante friends. Each of them was unique and would give me opposing advice on big life decisions. They gave me the love, support, and strength to navigate this "brutiful" crazy life. They, along with my mom, and my siblings were the good news call, the panic call, and the my-life-is-over-call.

That was who I was at that moment, but to figure out how I got there, I needed to go back to where it all began. I needed to understand why half of us in the boardroom felt the proposed solutions were insane and the other half felt they were the best solutions. What makes us the type of leaders we become? Why did I feel so strongly this was wrong?

SEASON ONE:

THE EARLY YEARS:
LOVE, LAUGHTER, DIVORCE,
DEATH, AND LOSS

THE BEGINNING:
WHERE IT ALL STARTED

I think our leadership styles, professional and personal, develop from our unique blend of life experiences through each season of our lives. A big part of our conscious and our unconscious belief systems are developed in our formative childhood years. We create *"Notes to Self"* that drive our macro life decisions and our everyday micro decisions. As I looked back on my first season, there were several key influences and events that shaped my personality and leadership style.

Note to Self

**We do not choose where we are born
or what family we are born into.
But what we take from it
and how we expand on it is all up to us.**

I grew up in the South to a middle-income family financially strained for most of my childhood years due to divorce but incredibly wealthy in love, laughter, and faith. Just my siblings, mom, nieces, and nephews made up 25 for Thanksgiving gatherings and when you extended to uncles, aunts and cousins, a family reunion meant 60-plus people. It was a big family. My parents divorced when I was young and somehow (miraculously) stayed good friends, a testament to my mom's forgiveness and kindness more than anything else. My family grounded me and taught me the importance of faith, humor, and acceptance of diverse personalities. My maternal side was American of English descent, raised in the East Tennessee suburbs with relations to two presidents, William and Benjamin Harrison. My paternal side was Cuban and Belgian with worldly stories of immigration from Africa and Europe. I took tremendous pride in my unique blend of DNA. I loved that it was different.

My parents' divorce was difficult to accept. My dad living eight hours away made it impossible for him to be a part of our daily lives. I lived with a recurring dream of my dad leaving us. I can't quite discern if it was an authentic memory or one my subconscious created. I was four years old, riding my tricycle up and down our driveway on Hickory Lane with my siblings. My mom watched the four of us laugh and giggle as we biked the driveway, creating obstacle courses with sticks and pinecones while playing 'chicken' as we pointed our bikes toward each other to see who would chicken out first. I was at the top of the driveway pausing to wave goodbye to Dad. His car was packed to its roof. He was heading to Lakeland, Florida to find us a house and start a new business venture. That was the story. My dad and I caught each other's eyes. I was expecting a smile and a quick wave before I returned to the fun. Instead, I saw fear and sadness, with a hint of guilt in his eyes that I had never seen before. I recognized all of that, even though I was so young. I had this feeling something wasn't right. I knew in my soul, in my intuition, that our lives were about to change. He was leaving us, and no one knew at that moment, except my intuition. My soul knew. My brain took over. It was too much to comprehend. My brain said get back to laughing and having fun. Ignore the feeling. Keep busy. It was what we did in my family. It was our survival technique—stay busy, maintain a sense of humor, and look forward to the future. Dear God, sweet little four-year-old girl, don't look back.

He telephoned from Florida asking for a divorce and mom did what she did best. She made lemonade out of lemons and leaned heavily on her faith.

Note to Self

**Sometimes, people I love move on and it feels unfair,
like pure abandonment.
Dads aren't always present for the daily stuff—
emotionally or physically.
Moms seem to carry the extra burden of home responsibilities
and making everything okay for others.**

The women in my family were strong and never complained. They made the best of the hand they were dealt and used humor as a stress reducer, health enhancer, and pain antidote. Witnessing my mom become a single parent unexpectedly and raise four kids was nothing short of miraculous. She modeled grace, integrity, forgiveness, optimism, and resilience. She is a light-skinned, blue-eyed blond, with the energy of ten people, a natural athlete, and the faith of Mother Teresa. She is light-hearted, funny, and buzzes around like a hummingbird, busy all the time. The epitome of southern hospitality, she gives more than receives. She welcomed my father and her former mother-in-law into our home for Thanksgiving and Christmas despite the divorce. I will be forever indebted to her for that gift. We had divorced parents, but we were able to preserve "traditional" family holidays with everyone under one roof, laughing and enjoying the holidays. My parents were both kind to each other and not once in my entire childhood did either of them say a negative comment about the other. The way they made each other laugh was simply a joy to witness and kept the typical divorce awkwardness at bay. My mother did her best balancing the masculine and feminine roles brilliantly, by default.

**Women are strong.
No matter the odds stacked against them,
they seem to overcome almost anything.**

In addition to my mom, my two grandmothers were amazing examples of perseverance, resilience, and adopting unique careers for their time. My paternal grandmother was a Cuban immigrant who left her family of nine siblings to come to America and study at age 14. Where do you get the courage to leave everything and move to a country where you don't even know the language? She became a college graduate and nearly finished her master's degree at a time when it was almost unheard of for women, much less a single immigrant woman from Cuba. As she was taking a course for her master's degree at Vanderbilt University, she fell in love with her professor, a young, astute Belgian man in the States for just a summer to teach. From her own description, they fell madly in love and married shortly after. The Belgian army called him to serve in Africa, specifically the Belgian Congo. After a long arduous ship ride to Africa, they settled in a small village where my father was born. My grandfather traveled with the Belgian army across Africa, fell ill and died in Egypt while on a mission. My grandmother got word as she was alone in Africa with a toddler and another child on the way. The love of her life was gone. She wasn't in Cuba. She wasn't in the United States. It was the 1940s. She went into the bathroom which I am sure was some sort of outhouse. Her intention was to kill herself as the grief was too much and the future was too hard. Then, my father, this little two-year-old toddler, knocked on the outhouse door, "Mamá, Mamá?" The wife and the widow would have ended her life, but the mother could not.

This is the story that I recall when I think I am having a difficult time in life. When I think I can't handle a certain situation. She found the strength to make her way back to the States, raise two boys, and have a highly regarded career. As a female college professor in the 1950s she faced many challenges that most likely make my challenges look like a cakewalk. Her more influential aspect was her joyful spirit and lack of any resentment. She chose to live a life of worldly travels, ballroom dancing, and siestas, all while managing a full-time career and being a single parent. She led herself out of crisis. She taught me that I can do hard things and I can do them joyfully.

My maternal grandmother had a very different life but was equally remarkable. She lived in the same small Southern town her entire life, married young and worked at home raising five children, until at age 65 when she decided to open a restaurant. Katty's Korner became a legendary breakfast and lunch diner where the local royalty chose to dine—the sheriff, bank president, local businessmen, and the church ladies. It was featured in Southern Living Magazine twice and multiple times in the local Kingsport paper. She was also named the honorary First Lady of Kingsport twice. Her "success" seemed to happen almost by accident. She didn't set goals or have a career track planned. She did it her way, breaking "proper" restaurant business regulations and accounting rules along the journey. She followed her common sense—if it didn't make sense to her, she didn't do it. She was blunt as hell, loved everyone, and had this rare ability to not worry. She just did what she loved and was one of the most unstressed, authentic people I knew.

All the women in my family before me were different in the best ways possible, hell-bent on taking life's knocks and just moving forward. None of them played the victim card. They were my first examples of leadership. I observed and took the pieces from each of them that would serve me well, but not all the pieces.

Note to Self

It's never too late to start or change careers.
I can make lemonade out of lemons,
no matter what the circumstances.
Try to take the high road and never play victim.

—————— ♀ ——————

THE BALLET DAYS:
WORK ETHIC AND PERFORMING

M y siblings and I each had our own identity. One was soccer. Another was swimming, and another was music. I was the ballerina. I never set out to be a ballerina, it happened by coincidence. A dear family friend was attending the university nearby and frequently came over for Sunday dinner. For four young kids, he was a college boy to wrestle and play endless basketball games.

One Sunday, he showed up with his beautiful girlfriend, who happened to be the prima ballerina of the Columbia City Ballet. I was maybe 8 years old and had never taken a ballet class. It was a foreign concept to me. My siblings and I were "performing" for her, which may or may not have included tumbling, goofy dancing, wrestling, and hanging from the door frame. At some point in that first meeting, she noticed something in me that triggered her to suggest to my mother that I try ballet.

This beautiful stranger, the prima ballerina and lead teacher at the ballet studio, became my first mentor. Since we were not able to afford ballet classes, she offered me a scholarship. I don't remember falling in love with ballet at the first lesson. I just remember finding myself in the midst of something out of my comfort zone and wanting to conquer its difficulty and meet her expectations of me. I remember feeling different than the other girls. I was from the other side of town, literally and figuratively. I realized quickly that most of them had been taking dance lessons since they were 2 or 3 years old, and many were from wealthier families. I didn't necessarily understand the value of the scholarship, I just knew I had to work hard to keep it, or I wouldn't be able to continue ballet. I also felt an inner whisper that I needed to work harder than the others to pay back the generosity as well as to catch up. So, I did.

Life presents opportunities at the most unexpected times.
Be ready. Say yes.
You can get "there" with money or hard work or both.
I only had one option. Hard work it is.

I honed my skill and rose in the ballet ranks to a soloist, performing in all the great classical ballets—the Nutcracker, Giselle, Romeo and Juliet, Swan Lake, and so many others. It was thrilling and I loved every moment of those ballet years. I thrived in the high demands and insane expectations of the ballet world. The daily intense workouts were heaven to me. The requirement to use, feel, and perfect every muscle in my body was addictive. The strength and muscle control required to deliver a perfect performance by making balancing and spinning on my toes look effortless was one of the greatest athletic challenges of my life. I embraced every aspect of it. I had this all-consuming relationship with the process of working hard, fine-tuning, and perfecting. The mindset was to do it better than I did yesterday— jump higher, spin faster, be more flexible. Every step, every move could always be better. There was always room for improvement.

The mirror, the weekly weigh-ins, the bleeding blisters, and the dieting were all part of the discipline. I remember the daily regimen of arriving home at 10 p.m. with bleeding toes after a full day of high school, 1 to 2 hours each of teaching ballet, taking ballet classes, and hours of rehearsing. My physical body was exhausted from head to toe, only matched by the mental exhaustion of memorizing choreography and keeping up with schoolwork. My raw, blistered toes would sting from being exposed to the air and then the nightly shower. The first drops of water would hit the raw blister and send a striking pain straight up my body. Then there was the post-shower routine. It was the worst. I would pour pure rubbing alcohol on each blister so a callous would quickly form overnight enabling me to squeeze my deformed, injured toes in those tight, wooden toe shoes again the next day. I drove my sisters and brother crazy screaming and waving my foot back and forth in the air to get through the unbearable pain. I learned something invaluable during this daily process for 12 years. The pain subsides within one or two minutes. I think this was one of my first lessons of what would become a lifetime philosophy, *this too shall pass.*

The ballet days instilled a work ethic in me that I didn't realize wasn't the norm until later in my career. I never took a sick day. I never missed a class or a rehearsal. If you missed a day you would tighten up and fall behind. Monday through Friday I went straight to the studio after school until late in the evening. Saturday and Sunday were even better because I had most of the day to put in longer hours of rehearsal without the burden of school. At the time, I didn't really care much about anything else.

Note to Self

This too shall pass. The pain passes.
Working hard can be fun and rewarding.
I can do hard.

—— 💡 ——

Fortunately, I never fell prey to the eating disorders rampant among ballet dancers at the time, but I did find myself practicing extreme dieting and sweating techniques with my peers. Saturday late morning was weigh-in. This meant a laxative for dinner Friday night, skipping breakfast Saturday and Saran Wrapping your stomach and thighs during Saturday morning class. I could easily sweat out 2 or 3 pounds if needed. Sweat made our tights and leotard heavy so on desperate days, we stripped down to our birthday suits before stepping on a scale. Every ounce mattered. We couldn't take any chances, or you might get cut. Unhealthy? Yes, but that didn't matter.

Our idols in the ballet world were some of the worst examples of health. Giselle Kirkland, one of the top ballerinas during my time, wrote in her autobiography about unsustainable eating habits for a highly impressionable audience, which included aspiring ballerinas like me. She allowed herself one apple a day cut in four squares while in rehearsals and performing the most demanding prima ballerina roles for hours. Insanity. I tried it for a few days, and successfully dropped some weight. I felt weak and didn't perform at my level of skill but received praise for my dieting efforts. Weight loss was complimented by all, indirectly encouraging us to continue our unhealthy techniques. I remember one summer while having the honor of training in New York City with David Howard and some of the other great ballet masters, I reached my lowest weight ever. Everyone assumed it was a deliberate result of dieting and training, but the truth was that I ran out of money.

Although I had somehow convinced my parents to let me go to New York City with two of my closest ballet friends unsupervised, my estimated costs fell short of reality. We stayed in a dormitory for models, actresses, and dancers, which kept the short-term rent low compared to normal New York options. We had guessed what our food costs would be to the best of our ability, but New York is expensive. I was running out of money by the last week, so I stuck with the free breakfast at the dormitory and maybe ate a granola bar in the afternoon. We were training several times a day. When I returned home, the toughest of my ballet masters, whose attention I craved the most, praised my appearance. It was one of only two times she ever truly praised me.

Note to Self

**Skinny feels good. Skinny gets praised.
Skinny gets attention.
Got to figure out how to be thin but be able to eat.**

———— ♀ ————

Performing on stage for over a decade gave me a mental edge, like many athletes, that stayed with me for a lifetime. There were so many fears I learned to overcome. I learned how to tame the stage fright and even enjoy the butterflies in my stomach and the adrenaline in my veins. Learning to be comfortable performing in front of hundreds of people for hundreds of performances was invaluable for my years as an executive in the corporate world. But even the smaller challenges and fears were life lessons. Like when we learned new lifts with our partners, which for the female meant high risk. I had to trust my male partner but we both had to fall many times before we got it right. Although the male dancers got hurt too, most of the time the female dancers were falling from high positions and suffering bruises in all the most tender parts, between the legs, armpits, thighs, and lower back. Like the weekly blisters, bruises were never given time to heal. You endured the pain and just kept going. As a ballerina, my pain tolerance had to be high, and I learned that the skills which were unattainable one week were attainable the next. It just took an insane number of attempts.

I remember rehearsing for my favorite role, the Arabian doll in the Nutcracker. My artistic director had choreographed a brilliant yet difficult lift that my partner and I were struggling to master. We were determined to get it right before we left that night. We rehearsed it over and over again. I can still hear his voice, "Again. Again. Almost. Again. Again." We finally got it.

I got home, stripped for the shower, and looked in the mirror. The entire upper left side of my body was black and blue. I smiled. I did it and my body would remember how to do it again tomorrow. My artistic director's ideas for this role seemed to expand. One year it was to spray paint my entire body gold from head to toe. Another year he rolled me up in a carpet as two male dancers carried me on stage. They would elegantly set me down as they kicked the carpet, rolled it out and I arose unfolded. It looked great on stage. The only problem is being rolled up in a tight carpet is quite a claustrophobic feeling. It took me months to be able to hold it together for the minutes it took to move from backstage through the opening. It was terrifying. Opening night, he knew my struggle. As we were about to go on stage and I was wrapped tightly in the carpet with my hands above my head, I heard him say, "Merde, Kristi, break a leg." I slowly stuck one hand out of the carpet and extended my middle finger. The backstage crew got a good laugh. The gold paint, which I am sure was toxic, lasted weeks post performances. A lifetime of memories made it all worth it.

Note to Self

**Never say you can't do something until
you have tried it at least a hundred times.
Almost anything is possible. Anything is "figureoutable."**

_____ ♀ _____

LIVING IN TWO WORLDS:
THE BENEFITS
AND THE HYPOCRISY

My ballet world was different from the rest of my life. I found myself not only dressed in beautiful costumes for performances but also in beautiful gowns at fundraising galas. There were fancy foods and drinks, and lots of wealthy donors. I was living a rich life without the corresponding bank account, immersed in the champagne and caviar lifestyle at a very young age, and I liked it. The other side of my reality was that we were living paycheck to paycheck back home. My two worlds were extremely different. We could barely afford the numerous toe shoes required to keep up with the demanding rehearsal and performance schedules. I remember having pairs of toe shoes lined up in my half of the room I shared with my sister. I would fold the flaps inside out and pour floor wax in the toe part and let them air out. If I rotated the pairs every few days, they lasted a little longer, saving a few dollars.

Ballet didn't just teach me to be an athlete and how to perform, it taught me to be resilient, fearless, determined, and adaptable. It also taught me the power of diversity and acceptance. The ballet world includes a higher-than-average number of gay men and women. Many of my closest ballet friends were gay. I loved them. In contrast at home, in church, and at my school, homosexuality was not accepted, nor was it really addressed. I remember sitting in church, hearing that homosexuality was a sin and those who practiced it would go to hell. In school even those we knew were gay didn't "come out" and few discussed it. The silence spoke volumes.

It was the 1980s and the HIV/AIDS epidemic was spreading. At the time, the medical community knew little about this deadly virus. They knew its transmission was predominantly among gay men, contracted through sexual partners and blood transfusions, but they didn't know how contagious it was through other types of contact. There was no cure at the time. One of our own, one of my dear friends and ballet partners, contracted HIV. He was talented, funny, and kind. He was scared and he was shamed. I was afraid for my friend and this fear was shared among all of us in our ballet family. Could we contract it? No one knew for sure. We were all together, all the time. Ballet was physical. We sweated and touched each other constantly. We loved him. Even in my ballet world, we didn't really talk about it. We just knew. The silence was both deafening and isolating.

Then there was the hate. It was palpable, especially in the southeast. The hatred toward gays and toward this virus was verbally expressed constantly. It made me sick. Christians were saying it was a disease sent from God to abolish the gays. They deserved it. How could someone say that? They didn't know Thomas. How could they hate someone they had never met? I was young, confused, and angry. It was unfair. I was a Christian, but I didn't feel that way. I thought we were supposed to love everyone. The Jesus I had read about would have been the first one to hold a sick ostracized human, just like he did with lepers. This judgment and alienation didn't make sense to me. The line between good and evil, conjured by my young 15-year-old mind in a world often presented as black and white, was getting blurry amid the hypocrisy.

My family went to church every Sunday. We attended a typical southern United Methodist church. Our youth leaders were some of the most influential people in my life. I adored them. Our youth group was a special group of humans. We went on ski trips, beach trips and camping retreats. The shenanigans and the laughter created special bonds. The people of the church were like family to us. And Thomas was like family to me. The dichotomy of my two worlds was difficult to understand and hard to accept. I ruminated over the contradictions in my head but rarely out loud. I was the only one living in both worlds, so who would understand?

Then what I feared most happened. Thomas' sickness progressed rapidly, and it wasn't long after his diagnosis that he lost his battle with this virus. We lost a friend and I mourned with my ballet family, but I couldn't even share the grief with my other world. They would never have understood. I knew they didn't want to understand. So, I didn't talk about it. Silence again.

Note to Self

Life is unfair. Silence seems like the only choice
but also feels like the wrong choice.
Seemingly good people can hate for the wrong reasons.
I don't want to be like that.

TRAJECTORY SHIFT:
MURDER, CANCER, AND COLLEGE

Being book smart, I was expected to go to college and get a good job, but at 18, I considered myself a dancer, and I expected to do it forever, even if that meant a move to New York City. My dad figured it was a short-term whim, but I was called to keep dancing. However, soon a factor appeared that outweighed my heart's desire.

Cancer. One word is all that disease deserves for acknowledgment. It feels like it targets the good ones; the ones we need so desperately standing next to us while we navigate our way through this world. Dad had Waldenstrom macroglobulinemia, a rare cancer that the medical community knew little about. Treatment was complex and success was rare. When my dad told us his news, there was no internet, and little medical research on this type of cancer. We didn't know what we didn't know. Dad was mid-40s and in remission, but it could come back at any time. He had first been diagnosed years earlier when he felt severely fatigued after a 5K race. His initial blood work confirmed he was anemic but other symptoms encouraged the doctor to run more tests. He had chosen not to tell us then and went through chemo and radiation treatments alone. Living our daily lives eight hours away from him there was no way for us to have noticed. He was a workaholic real estate manager in Florida. He went to the hospital at 6 a.m., got his treatment and went right into the office. He had no side effects. Why didn't he tell us? We were his kids. Didn't we have a right to know? That damned silence again. Why don't people talk about big things, big feelings? I was mad. I was scared. Dad was one of my idols.

Since my parents were divorced, my time with my father was limited and precious, which made me crave more. He was tall, dark, and handsome. His looks got attention, but it was his charisma and humor that drew people to him. His presence just made you want to be near him. He would have a room full of people laughing within minutes. He appeared, to this young girl, to be the whole package. To me, there was God ... then there was my mom and my dad. From my perspective, they were almost equal, but then again that's true of most little girls. My dad and I understood each other. We had similar characteristics from physical appearance to work ethic. I observed and I learned from his choices and his regrets.

Given the cancer news, I decided to blow up my ballet dreams and go to college in Tampa, one hour from my dad. I was giving up my love, my ballet family, and going somewhere where I didn't know anyone to do something—attend college—that I had no desire to do. All because my dad had cancer, and I wanted to be near him. My heart was breaking into a thousand pieces. Every cell in my body didn't want to go. Physically, I was a wreck. Saying goodbye to my boyfriend, dog, family, ballet friends, and ballet world was the hardest thing I had done in my life to that point. My intuition was saying stay, but I had already committed to the University of South Florida and my dad was thrilled. I felt obligated. I felt it was the "smart" thing to do. My freshman year of college was the most miserable I have ever been in my life.

**When I go against my intuition,
my body will physically revolt.
Sometimes the "smart" decision
is the wrong decision.**

———— ○ ————

    I chose to major in marketing and minor in business. I met some great friends, and made the best of my college situation, but I didn't want to be there. I found the best ballet master in the area and took and taught classes with her my freshman year to keep a little bit of dance in my life while in college, but I was no longer performing. I was miserable. I wanted my full ballet performing world back. Instead, the cancer came back.

    Dad and I had enjoyed being close to each other. We got to do so many things that were never possible before. We would meet for dinner, go out on the boat, and I would even come "home" to his place to do laundry and visit. It was surreal and having that one-on-one time with him was priceless. In a big family, there are great rewards and amazing times, but the one thing you never get when you are one of four children is much solo time with a parent. We were always sharing his attention in our limited time with him. Those two years when it felt like I had his undivided attention, the long conversations were invaluable, especially considering what happened next.

    My junior year in college, I made a trip back to New York City with my then boyfriend whose family lived outside of the city. I was nervous about leaving Dad, but he was stable and insisted it was no big deal. We arrived in the big city and hopped on the subway to explore the sights. I hadn't been back in the city since the summer I trained there for ballet. Floods of memories and great times came back to me. I talked ninety miles an hour about where the ballet studio had been, where I'd seen Mikhail

Baryshnikov and where we had lived on 87th Street in the dorm. I told him how I had been a young, naive 15-year-old living in New York with my two best ballet friends. There were two to a room. I drew the short straw and got the room with a stranger. I looked around and saw my new roommate's pictures and decor. It looked like she was a model and actress. Shortly after, she came bouncing in the room with a huge smile and introduced herself as Rebecca Schaeffer. She had curly auburn hair. She was adorable and kind. It didn't take long before we told each other our short life stories and became fast friends.

Rebecca had a recurring role on the daytime soap opera, "One Life to Live," and had success as a model on the cover of Seventeen magazine and a stint in Japan. She was worldly compared to me and was my New York City guide of what to do and what not to do. We both had intense schedules. I was training and she had to be on set in the wee hours of the early morning. One of my craziest nights in New York City was with Rebecca. It was getting late and neither of us could sleep. Rebecca had one of her biggest scenes the next day and had to be on set at 6 a.m. The girls and I had an early ballet class. Rebecca and I decided to take a walk to see if we could wear ourselves out. It was midnight and I might have been young and naive, but I knew it wasn't a good idea for two young girls to be walking about the city late at night.

The walk wasn't tiring us, and we were thirty blocks from the dorm. We turned a corner and found ourselves in the middle of a crowd. It wasn't a party. It was just a large group of about forty individuals hanging out on the street. They looked kind of rough, and I felt nervous. Two seconds later, we heard, "It's a bust," then, "NYPD. Freeze." We were in the middle of a New York City drug bust and we were innocent. The cops were on the far side of the crowd, so Rebecca and I looked at each other, turned and ran. We didn't say a word the whole time. We never looked back. It must have been a full sprint, my personal record, I assure you. We ran into the dorm straight to our room, collapsed on our twin beds, and laughed our asses off. Holy cow, we could have ended up in jail for walking. Can you imagine me, a 15-year-old little southern girl, calling my parents from a jail in New York City?

Rebecca, originally from Eugene, Oregon, had been out on her own for a while and her parents supported her trying to "make it" if there was continued progress. She was so confident and independent. I adored her and felt so lucky to have had a summer with her. Saying goodbye to Rebecca was hard. Back in those days, there were no cell phones and long-distance calls were expensive. We knew staying in touch was going to be difficult, but we were going to try.

We wrote a few letters over the next few years, and I watched with pride as Rebecca started making it as an actress. She moved out to LA and got the supporting role of Patti on the sitcom "My Sister Sam" with Pam Dawber. I couldn't believe it. Rebecca was on primetime and in a show with the "Mork and Mindy" star. She was someone. Then, she got a few roles in movies, including Dyan Cannon's "The End of the Innocence." A shining young actress making her way. It was so much fun to watch and couldn't have happened to a nicer person.

Note to Self

**Life delivers unexpected people
when you least expect it.
Enjoy the chance meetings
and be fully present for the experience.**

My boyfriend, supportive and a little exhausted from all my storytelling, stopped me to say the next stop was ours. As we exited the subway, we walked right in front of a news stand. The headline read, "Actress, 21, Is Shot and Killed After She Opens Front Door. Rebecca Schaeffer." *What? This must be a movie she is in. No, this can't be Rebecca. Murdered? I'm in New York City where we lived together. This can't be happening. Rebecca is in LA. Rebecca is 21. It says 21 in the headline. The subheading says her name. Are there two Rebecca Schaeffers?*

The noisy subway hustle and bustle got quiet. I couldn't hear anything or anyone. I couldn't think. I couldn't comprehend. *This can't be happening. This can't be true.* The newspaper had to be wrong. Please God, not Rebecca. Who would ever murder Rebecca? She was one of the kindest souls I had ever met. She was just now, after years of hard work, getting a break in the relentlessly difficult acting industry. She was just now starting to become an actress everyday people recognized. How could this be happening?

I don't know how long I stood there dumbfounded. I don't know what my boyfriend said to get me to speak. I remember just pointing to the newspaper and reading it and rereading it. I couldn't even see the whole article through the newsstand. I collapsed in his arms and just kept saying "murdered" over and over. Things like this didn't happen in my world.

Rebecca's death was tragic for so many reasons. There is much that has been written about it publicly as it was a celebrity murder and it triggered better protection laws for celebrities and public figures from obsessed fans. The short version of her horrific murder is an obsessed fan went to her residence. He rang the doorbell, she answered in her robe, and he shot and killed her. Her murder is not my story to tell.

How a murder of a friend impacted me *is* my story to tell. The unfairness of the murder left an imprint on my life that is difficult to put into words. She was a year older than me. We were in our 20s, just getting started in our careers. It woke me up. It broke my heart. It provoked a sense of urgency that I still feel. Societal norms and expectations are all based on one significant assumption: that we live into our 60s, 70s, or 80s. Rebecca's early death, very clearly, taught me that assumption is fiction. What if I only had one more year to live? How would I plan my life? What would I do differently?

The randomness of her death haunted me. Rebecca was safe at home, or so she thought. It wasn't like she was at a large event with crazy fans everywhere. She was in her robe at home and answered the doorbell. "Life is dangerous" became part of my subconscious belief system. Rebecca wasn't even that famous. Most didn't know her name. She didn't walk around with security in fear for her life. There were so many other famous celebrities. Why her?

The next several days, I was somewhat lost. I didn't know how to process or grieve Rebecca's murder. My family and friends didn't know her. I had not spoken to her in a year. I couldn't go to the funeral. I didn't have her parents' contact information. I was an island. Trying to process, I remember talking to my mom briefly, but really I didn't speak much about it with anyone. I had some lonely cries. I had some spiritual conversations with Rebecca. I don't think I ever really took the time to truly grieve her death. I just kept going. I got lost in busyness, the way so many of us bury the things in life we don't want to deal with. After all, my dad was battling cancer. I had to focus on him.

Note to Self

**Life is really unfair. Life is short.
Death can happen at any time
and is out of my control.
I need to do everything now.
Compartmentalizing grief and carrying on
might not be the best, but it is all I know how to do.**

Dad was still working and doing everything he could to keep things normal while receiving his second round of chemo and radiation treatments. It was the beginning of my junior year of college and my younger sister had joined me at USF as a freshman.

We all assumed the treatments would work like last time and Dad would win his battle.

Then he lost his hair from the chemo. That was the worst day. I drove over to his office with the idea of cheering him up. I walked in. He was wearing a wig. I tried not to react, but it didn't look right. It shocked me. My handsome, charismatic dad had not just lost his hair, but his physical body was starting to look sickly. He was visibly shaken. I had acted on stage a hundred times. I could pretend everything was okay. I could stop the tears that so badly wanted to surface. But the inevitable was coming. I quickly told him to finish up his work and that I was going to run to the store. We would meet back at the house for dinner. I will never forget speed walking out of his corner office, down the hallway, then beginning to run as the tears came heavily down my cheeks. I had to get out the exit door before the ugly cry started. I couldn't let him hear me gasping for breaths or the loud guttural sounds that weren't going to stop for an hour.

Dad didn't look like my dad anymore. That was the first time I thought he might die. That night, we had a bald head party, and I shaved his head. His best friend came over, and we worked on styling the two wigs. We laughed trying to make light of the worst day of Dad's life. We took pictures of him bald, with a baseball hat, with wig one and wig two. We all decided he looked best and felt most comfortable bald or bald with a baseball hat. There was no use in trying to hide it at work. So, he made the brave decision to tell his staff the next morning. He, like always, added a little humor as he delivered the news of his cancer, and it went off without a hitch (or should I say without a hair). He mustered a different kind of courage that day. The man that had it all was losing one of his greatest assets. Cancer sucks.

Note to Self

Health changes everything.
When someone is battling a disease,
it disrupts their entire life
and their loved ones' lives.
I need to understand how to prevent cancer.

WITNESSING GRACE
IN LEADERSHIP
AND CHOOSING BUSYNESS

My father's health continued to decline over the next couple of months. It felt like it happened quickly, but I am not sure of the exact timeline as I know he hid a lot of his symptoms from me and everyone else. He would bring his briefcase to the hospital and pretend he was fine and work from his bed. Then the second he was released he would race back to the office, and it was business as usual. He was in and out of the hospital several times before I got the dreaded call. He had hallucinated during a district meeting with fellow managers, and they called an ambulance. It was bad this time and we needed to get there quickly.

My younger sister and I raced to the hospital, an indescribable feeling. The car just would not go fast enough. We knew we must get there, but at the same time, we didn't want to get there because what we were about to experience was what none of us wanted. The smell of the hospital makes me nauseous still to this day. I hate hospitals. The clinical smell, the number of sick people, the sadness of those there to see their sick people, the sound of the machines, all make me want to vomit. For me, hospitals are where people die. A hospital is where my dad died on that September day in 1989. I was 20.

He left too young, too soon, before my college graduation, before I met my husband, before I got married, before I had kids, before I became the person I am today. The void, the black hole, was so deep it seemed to take out all the light that used to shine so brightly in our family. We were a happy, fun family. Would we ever get that back? The sadness was so intense that it felt as if it became part of my bones or even deeper, part of my marrow.

I carried the pain with me every step. There were times I remember thinking I couldn't make it through another day. I remember literally feeling pains in my heart and thinking, is this what they call heartache? I wore sunglasses for what seemed like an eternity because eye contact with anyone would cause a flood of uncontrollable tears.

It took me months to say the words, "My father passed away." I dialed his phone number repeatedly just to hear his voicemail. I had never lost someone so close to me. Thomas was a friend. Losing him was heart wrenching, so I thought. Rebecca was murdered. It was shocking. It was unfair, but I grieved from afar. This was my dad. I needed him. I didn't know everything yet. I had life questions that I needed him to answer for me. I needed him to teach me about the stock market, life insurance, job choices, and the other 10 million subjects I was going to come across in my life.

The funeral was surreal. What struck me was who showed up and who didn't. Those who were merely acquaintances stood by our sides offering unlimited emotional support. People we never knew came to pay their respects and help us. Some of our closest friends did not show up. They didn't know what to say. It is what people do with death. Some can't participate. I promised myself that day, I would show up for others even if it was just a note. Even if we don't know what to say, we just need to let them know we're thinking of them.

One of my bosses from Outback Steakhouse, where I was a waitress, attended the funeral. She and my manager at Outback

Steakhouse were two of the greatest bosses I could ask for during that season of my life. They both had high expectations as managers and demanded excellence but also had compassion. She hugged me and said, "Take as much time as you need but don't take more than you need. Your Outback family will be there to help you through. We miss you." I never forgot her kindness and support. My entire Outback work family was amazing. I didn't know what to do. I didn't know how much time I "should" take off. I didn't understand this world.

Note to Self

**Be there for others in the awkward times.
Show up even if it is just a short note
or a brief call. Saying nothing or doing nothing
should never be the choice.**

You become different after a life experience like death. You mature years in one moment of time. You find a reservoir of strength that you didn't know you had. You take responsibility for things you never had to before. You view the world differently. Life becomes a temporary state, one that can be taken away at any given moment. You deal more in the moment, just one moment at a time. You make deals with yourself. "If I can make it for the next two minutes without crying then it will be better than yesterday, and I can tell everyone I am doing better." Because deep down in your soul, you know all the hundreds of people asking you how you are doing really don't want to hear the truth of your insane pain. It's easier to simply say, "I'm doing better, thank you."

I went back to college classes and tried to go through the motions. One of my professors, head of the department, looked me in the eye during class. Somehow, he knew. I went to his office after class. I needed to understand how I could make up the two weeks I had been out. I tried to speak but couldn't. The tears just flooded down my face. He handed me a tissue box and said, "Take your time." Then he pulled out my dad's obituary newspaper clipping. He said what I couldn't. "I'm so sorry to hear about your loss. Losing a parent is hard. What can we do to help?"

I mustered a few words about the need to make up assignments. He asked, "Are you sure you want to come back this semester? You have options." It had never occurred to me that I had options. I never thought about taking time off. I told him I wanted to try to come back and catch up. I did, but I couldn't concentrate. I ended up dropping out that semester as I was already ahead in college credits and could still graduate on time.

The compassion of professors and bosses during this time were giving me early examples of leadership. The kindness of family, friends and strangers when going through the death of a loved one is what carried me. The alone time is lonely but there were just days where I couldn't be around people and the fetal position on the bathroom floor was all I could handle. I did need a little time to figure this all out.

Note to Self

**Good managers and people in leadership
positions can be compassionate
while at the same time demanding excellence.
Leaders can be human
and lead well all at the same time.**

Then that thing called time went by. I literally ran out of tears or reached pure exhaustion from crying so much. I realized no matter how much I cried, it wouldn't bring him back. I grew tired of being sad. At first, I caught myself smiling at a child in the store. Then I surprised myself as I heard my own laugh come back. Ever so slowly, I started remembering the good times instead of replaying the last few moments before Dad's death. I began going through the physical motions of my life—work, school, and friends. I interacted but I knew, and others knew, I wasn't totally present yet. Life goes on, and slowly, very, very slowly I joined the dance of life, albeit as a different version of myself. At some point, I recognized that the pain will never really leave me, but I had a choice to make. I could focus on the pain, or I could focus on the ordinarily amazing twenty years of love, laughter, joy, and fatherly advice. I chose the latter.

My gratitude for what I had began to overpower my loss. My father's life and his untimely death made me a better person— stronger, smarter, and more empathetic to others. His death gave me courage I wouldn't have had otherwise. I had survived the unthinkable, surely nothing life threw at me could hurt this bad again, I thought. Losing my father taught me the importance of being present with everyone I love because I know there is no guarantee I will have them tomorrow. It also changed the trajectory of my life toward a business career.

Note to Self

**Death feels like the ultimate abandonment.
It can change the trajectory of a person's life.**

I pivoted from dance and college to pure college and career. I don't remember consciously choosing to give up dance completely. I remember still yearning to go back home to family and my ballet world, but I didn't. I wonder why I didn't give myself permission to transfer colleges, go back to performing, and move back home when I wanted to so badly. Instead, I went full speed ahead toward financial security and career. I had to take care of myself now. I went into hyperdrive with an insane sense of urgency, a need to be the problem solver, an overachiever, and adopted an intense focus on health and a desire for success. It's time for real life adulthood.

Reality versus perception is a quintessential issue that we glimpse in hindsight but rarely get in the moment. The beliefs I adopted weren't right or wrong. They were my way of coping. My family role models, managers, and even the professor I had in the early years influenced my decisions, work ethic, and eventually my leadership style as an executive and as a parent.

SEASON TWO:

WORKING MOM LIFE:
EARLY CAREER, MARRIAGE, AND KIDDOS

THE HUSTLE AND THRILL
OF EARLY CAREER

The energy. The adrenaline. The intensity. The drive. The fun. The excitement. The potential.

The early years of my career had all this and more. My career began at an advertising agency. I'd interned there while in college and then was "awarded" an entry level job in my 20s. I say awarded as it was such low pay that I had to keep working as a bartender at Outback Steakhouse to pay rent. I was the grunt—the lowest ranking person in the agency. I backed up the receptionist on her lunch break. I answered phones. I helped every department with anything they needed—production, media, creative, traffic, or account service. It was high paced and deadline oriented.

The marketing world in the '90s was different from today's digital world. Communication was via fax and telephone, and the channels were outdoor boards, sports marketing, trade shows, newspaper, radio, and television. There was not one marketing automation software to help marketers when I got into the business. Today there are thousands.

The marketing channels have changed and targeting capability is dramatically improved. Today, there are more channels to reach our prospects like social media, online ads, apps, and streaming services. Marketers can create omnichannel marketing strategies with artificial intelligence and data unification. We can target communication via one-to-one, geofencing, behavioral, and so much more. Consumers are far more sophisticated and have greater power in holding brands accountable. They want to be entertained, feel connected to a brand, participate in creating content, and favor purpose-driven brands. Marketers must know their customers better than the customers know themselves and anticipate future market trends. Chief Marketing Officers are now transformational leaders in organizations.

Everything has changed yet the principle of marketing has stayed the same. At its simplest, marketing is creating a compelling story to a target audience and stakeholders, packaged in a way that it entices them to become raving fans of a product through purchase and referral.

In the 90s, advertising agencies were focused on ads in the key channels of newspaper, radio, television, and outdoor. The agency job was my first career job post-college, or what is commonly referred to as the "first real job." I've always hated that term, the first "real" job. It's so insulting. I have been working since I was 14 years old. What defines a real job? I was a ballet teacher for years. Then I worked at restaurants as a hostess, waitress, and bartender all through college. How was this my first real job? This was the beginning of a long struggle for me with societal definitions. My restaurant jobs would be invaluable later in my career when I became CMO of restaurant management software companies. I would end up speaking and doing media interviews about the value of restaurant jobs and how I felt everyone should have to work in a restaurant job to teach them hustle, customer service, and work ethic. There is nothing like working in hospitality.

Note to Self

Every job is valuable.

I was a bartender at Outback, where I had started out as a waitress when they first opened their doors in Tampa, Florida as a two-restaurant chain before they became Bloomin Brands, a $4 billion-plus global multi-chain restaurant holding company. The original partners were experienced entrepreneurs from other successful restaurant franchises. I worked side-by-side in the beginning days with some of the finest business people I had ever met then or since.

This is where I fell in love with the entrepreneurial spirit and learned the value of creating a phenomenal employee culture and producing a high-quality product at a fair price. Outback created customer fans, repeat business, and loyalty. I observed the brilliance of the partnership of the original four, three men and one woman. Each partner had a unique role and contributed a distinct value to the company. There was the fun-loving, carefree, brilliant chef. There was the more reserved financial and operational genius. Then there was the growth engine and visionary, and the people person, the trainer. This was where I first witnessed diversity at the top that worked. Diversity delivered greater business outcomes because they each contributed their zone of brilliance. I didn't realize at the time how unique this was to see a powerful female at the top and it was a long time before I saw someone like her again.

The high regard for operational excellence and product quality made serving at Outback Steakhouse a pleasure. A great product is everything. It makes customer service easier. It creates a powerful, organic referral growth mechanism. It makes being an employee a delight. It made me not want to leave, but I gave in to societal expectations and got a "real" job using my college degree.

I loved both the agency and the hospitality world. I loved learning and I absolutely adored meeting people along the way. These friendships always improved my world. Work was not just work. It was an unexpected joy that I was blessed to discover early on. Some of my lifelong friendships started then.

Note to Self

**Working hard and making money is thrilling.
I love the people I meet through work.
I've got to follow this career path. This could be great.**

The ad agency was my first salaried experience. Even though my salary was close to minimum wage, I was receiving a paycheck every two weeks. I had insurance and a 401K. I felt like I was an adult and now I needed to make smart financial decisions.

I immersed myself in financial books and seminars and I tried to learn everything I could about business. I read hundreds of self-help books and listened to every motivational speaker. I couldn't get enough of it. Self-teaching became a lifelong pursuit of mine. It satisfied my curiosity, gave me wisdom, and made me feel overprepared in life.

I did every job in the agency. I arrived early and stayed late. I asked questions, but more importantly I observed and listened. I watched the creative director and the graphic artists. I watched the production manager and the media buyer. I watched the partners. I couldn't get enough of soaking in as much knowledge as possible. I noticed how each department and individual had a different skill set. Like the way the four partners at Outback each contributed something different, the agency partners did as well. I noted how important the chemistry of a leadership team was to business success. Everyone must know their lane and when a bad egg gets in the mix, everything goes to hell in a handbasket.

The agency partners were brilliant entrepreneurs. I watched as they created new businesses to solve their clients needs. When courier services couldn't keep up with our demand, they created a new courier business that met our needs. One client was dissatisfied with their fulfillment warehouse vendor, so they created another business, a fulfillment warehouse with higher standards. Entrepreneurs create businesses to solve problems and leapfrog existing businesses that are not meeting the needs of the marketplace. It was fascinating to witness.

The entrepreneur business lessons, and my financial self-study gave me such a head start. The surprising concepts I learned in my 20s were extremely valuable. For example, I learned that you could become a millionaire by just putting away money at an early age, and real estate, with the right timing, was a good investment strategy. I put away as much as possible in savings on a very meager salary. I was single and all I needed was basic food, clothing, and shelter. My take home pay was so ridiculously low that it was technically below minimum wage. I also inherited a small amount of money from my father that I used as a down payment to buy a condo when I was 22. My self-study had told me to buy not rent and get a roommate to pay half the mortgage. So that is what I did. I was scared to death signing those papers. I was a young woman and knew what I was doing but didn't know what I was doing all at the same time. It took all the courage I could muster to go through with it, but I did it. It wasn't all ideal as you can only do the best you can with what you have at the time. The condo was in the "not so good" part of town, because that was what I could afford. My boyfriend at the time (future husband) had his car vandalized repetitively upon visits. I made it work.

Note to Self

Fear will always be there.
When I muster the courage to face my fear
and do it anyway, it is empowering.
Financial wisdom: save early, invest,
and always live below my means
regardless of my salary level.

Observing other employees in the business world was insightful. Many came in, did their job, and left. I took the time to understand the business model. How does the business earn money? How does the business lose money? How does your role impact the company? When you understand these simple concepts, then you can make an impact no matter where you are in the company hierarchy. Find the most significant pain point and do everything you can to help solve it, right where you are, before you ever get a promotion.

I did witness many "easy street" promotions. They always happened through the male network and at the time, that was usually at the golf course, in church, or at a bar. What I would learn later to call The Boys' Club. It didn't seem as unfair then as it does to me now in hindsight. It just seemed odd. I would watch a conversation lead to a promotion without an interview and without the person having the necessary experience for the job. Why put someone in a job who doesn't have the skill set? Who does that serve?

The result was always incompetence, without exception. I was fascinated to watch incompetence being excused. "Oh, that is just Todd being Todd. You are just going to have to do it yourself." The person didn't have the skill set or the experience to be in the job and then was allowed to stay in the job and excused from properly doing it. It was truly unbelievable. If someone does not earn a promotion or develop the muscles for a promotion, they can't excel. If someone is in a position and not performing, spend some time coaching them, but if they can't manage the job, let them go. Otherwise, it's a disservice to the person and those that work with them.

I also observed several talented, powerful women in key positions who may not have had the titles of the top positions but were instrumental in making the business work. They were exceptionally good at what they did. The top two creative talents under the creative director were women. These two were the ones that helped us win the NHL Tampa Bay Lightning account with the infamous "Kick Ice" slogan they developed. The best account executive was a woman. The kick ass production manager was a woman. The head of accounting was a woman. They weren't the partners, but they had a significant impact on the business and on me. My soul received a whisper. Keep going. There is a place for you.

Here is what I came to understand. The more obstacles and challenges a person endures on their way to the top, the more skills they acquire. They learn to be creative, innovative, communicate better, and overcome bias, which leads them to have refined skill sets by the time they get to the top. If a person is "gifted" a job with little to no experience and never held accountable to develop the skills required for a job, then they will most likely be incompetent in the job.

Note to Self

**Learn the business models
and find a way to make an impact.
There are great leaders and incompetent leaders.
Learn what to do from the great ones
and learn what not to do from the incompetent ones.
Tough times create strong humans.**

———— ○ ————

I thought I would stay in the advertising agency world my whole career. It was an adrenaline junkie's heaven. I thrived in the deadline and pressured-filled atmosphere and absolutely loved the creative process of innovative ads that resonated with consumers and delivered financial results for clients. I settled into the account services side of the agency business and learned from one of the best. She was brilliant at communicating with the partners, the creative team, and with the demanding clients. She had a gift. She was smart and independent. She was "successful" by many definitions. She had a home on the intercoastal waterway and seemed to be genuinely happy. I learned so much from her, but she was not married, and she had chosen not to have kids. Did this mean I couldn't have a great career, good marriage and have children? Was it impossible or was it possible, I wondered.

I also had my first experience with the good old fashioned "teach-those-young'uns-a-lesson" style leadership at the agency job. One of the partners felt it was his duty to make things difficult for me and hold me back. It was obvious to everyone in the agency. He degraded me with tasks that prevented me from making a real contribution. I guess his ego gained some satisfaction. Frustrating talented people creates unnecessary animosity that doesn't benefit the culture, or the company. But it did teach me what I didn't want to be like as a manager.

I had asked the partner if I could be assistant broadcast producer under the creative director for television commercials and was laughed out of his office. He said, "I will give you this, you got balls, but you don't have any experience." I countered with, "How can I have experience until you give me the opportunity?" I didn't get anywhere. So, I took my career into my own hands and decided to invest in "experience." I took my week of vacation and spent my hard-earned money on a broadcast training workshop at UCLA in California.

Note to Self

**Take things into my own hands. Always ask.
The worst that can happen is they say no.**

———— ♀ ————

This was my first travel alone experience. It sounded glamorous. Fly to LA by myself, stay on UCLA campus and get one step closer to learning what it takes to be a broadcast producer. I was scared. What was I thinking? The answer was I wasn't thinking, I was just doing. I was moving forward. I was going for it. I was just figuring it out as I went.

The LA trip was wonderful and disastrous all at the same time. LA opened my eyes to a whole different world much as NYC had during my ballet years. Big city life was exciting. The UCLA campus was beautiful. I learned about being a producer in a few days, but I fell ill with the flu. My fever was high. The head of the program drove me to the LA hospital. The HIV scare was still significant. The medical community talked relentlessly about the two ways HIV was transmitted, through sexual interaction or intravenously. LA was a hotspot for HIV and when I woke up in an LA hospital with an IV in my arm and alone, I was terrified. How had I gotten myself into this predicament? I should have played it safe. I should just chill like everyone else. But I didn't. There was something in my DNA. I always had felt the urge to push myself to be better, to learn, and to experience new environments. I always had to do it differently.

I was only in the hospital one night. I didn't need a blood transfusion, only some electrolytes. I finished the course and made my way back home to Tampa with a broadcast certification in my hand. I was a little bit wiser and a little bit more worldly, and I liked it.

It's funny how our minds always go to the worst-case scenario. Why don't we ever go to the best-case scenario? That was a thought that would continue to come up for me throughout my early years and it was a skill set I would not learn to apply until my 40s.

Note to Self

Exploring and experiencing new environments is exhilarating, but if I don't have my health, it negatively impacts everything.

———— ○ ————

THE BIG CORPORATE BEHEMOTH: BUILDING LEADERSHIP MUSCLES IN MIDDLE MANAGEMENT

An opportunity came up for me through the agency, but not *for* the agency. As a junior account executive, I worked on some great accounts. We had a top national airline, top national rental car companies, an up-and-coming national burger franchise and GTE Wireless, now Verizon Wireless. We were the advertising agency for GTE Wireless' Florida, Texas, and Pacific regions. Our client contact in the Florida region was going on maternity leave and had an opening for a marketing coordinator. She offered me the job. This was a big career decision for me as I loved the agency world and the small no rules entrepreneurial aspect of it. I didn't know if I'd like the client side. I had never worked in a large corporation. The red tape, bureaucracy, politics, and the company's behemoth size of GTE Wireless didn't appeal to me. But it was a significant pay raise, stock options, and far better benefits. I took it and it changed my career trajectory. I also left the agency on good terms, and they made a point to say I was welcome back anytime. I felt I had a fallback plan.

Note to Self

**Career decisions are difficult and risky.
Be open to all opportunities.
Plan but don't plan too much.
It is always a good idea
to leave a job on good terms.**

————— ♀ —————

Media spokesperson for press inquiries was part of my new role, and the first month on the job we were hit with a lawsuit. Just the day before, my boss had casually mentioned something about a customer in St. Petersburg who was suing the company claiming one of our cell phones had caused his brain tumor. The claim seemed ridiculous, so we didn't give it much attention. The next morning, I arrived in my little corporate cubicle and dialed into my voicemail to find it was "full" of 100-plus voicemails from different media outlets. The story had gone national, and everyone wanted a comment. I had my voicemail on speaker phone and was trying to write down every message while a million thoughts ran through my head on how I was going to handle this situation. My boss walked by as "voicemail number 85" was playing. I mouthed, "Help." We went into public relations crisis management, which I had studied in school but had never managed in real life. It was intense, and my boss was with me every step of the way. We called in the corporate headquarter big guns, and we handled the storm as well as could be expected. We were honest and responsive, which gained us great respect with our customers and the local community.

Note to Self

**Crisis management is scary and intense.
With honesty, authenticity, the right boss
and team, you can overcome anything.**

GTE taught me leadership skills. It was a $20 billion telecom giant and the third largest publicly held telecom company at the time. The parent company was a monopoly, meaning it had no competition in most of its business units, such as landline business, yellow pages, long distance, etc. The GTE Wireless business unit where I worked was the exception. We were in a heated, competitive battle and we were the young rebel division. The parent company was the epitome of old-school thinking and corporate bureaucracy. Being naive of the corporate rules and ways served me well in the sense that I just did what I thought was right and worked hard.

The company had a strong executive training program for its up-and-coming executives. The company offered courses in negotiation, management, finances and so much more. They paid for continuing education outside of the company and I took full advantage of all of it. I met and learned from some brilliant people whose wisdom and energy I could absorb while selectively adopting their best traits. In the wireless business unit, we were innovative, fiercely competitive, and rebellious. My bosses supported trying different ideas. We moved at lightning speed, worked long hours, and had an absolute blast. The bottom-line financial success reflected the brilliance of the team. There were so many A players. It was the perfect combination of an unlikely pairing of diverse people and just the right amount of competitive pressure, high standards, and leadership support.

I was just one component as the head of advertising, public relations, sports marketing, and events. The leadership pushed me with extremely high expectations, encouraged creativity and allowed me to fail. I learned some lessons, but they didn't let me fall so hard it was damaging. They led by example, and I was a willing student.

Yes, most of my bosses were men, I only had one female boss in my ten years at the company. They all taught me something different. They were all intelligent, kind, giving, and successful.

As I look back on the wireless team, I see the diversity, which I believe was all by accident, a result of hiring the best candidates for the jobs, as there were no inclusivity policies at the time. There was a mix of MBA academics, college-only grads, high school-only grads, White, Hispanic, Black and Asian Americans, and an openly gay man. It was the 1990s. This was rare. We were all considered middle management level. One of my bosses was an African American man. He was brilliant. We connected in a way that allowed me to learn more from him. Maybe it was because we were both minorities, or maybe we were just more alike personality wise. I'm not sure. Over half of middle management was women. Our top sales and service retail managers were women, and the top revenue store was run by a woman. She was confident, blunt, and brilliant. This was diversity but at the time I didn't even realize it. We worked extremely well together. We all collaborated and respectfully argued openly. The creative ideas that came out of this team were incredible. It was like our different perspectives and work ethics fed off each other. We were also all relatively young and hungry. We worked long hours willingly. We worked hard and played hard together. We created stellar bottom line success for the company. We weren't concerned with perfectionism, we were focused on results, speed, and action. I wonder now if diversity was our superpower. Was it the intelligence level of everyone on the team? Was it that we were all young and hungry? Was it that we all respected each other and got along both professionally and personally? What was the magic? Maybe it was all of those qualities. In contrast, as I looked "up" at top management, I noticed there was no diversity.

I thought this was the new normal in a work environment and it was amazing. Little did I know what I was part of back then just happened to be rare. As I moved "up" the corporate ladder, there was less and less diversity.

Note to Self

**There is endless success possible
when you have great leadership,
a diverse team, A players, and the freedom to be
innovative and creative
without worrying about being perfect.**

Transitioning from an individual contributor job to managing people is one of the most difficult career transitions for most of us. As an individual, you are responsible for yourself and your responsibilities, and when challenges arise you seek direction from your boss. As a manager, you are responsible for your tasks plus managing everyone else. You have the daily tasks, but you also must dedicate time to longer term strategic issues like budget, personnel recruitment and management, and cross department relationships. As a manager, you become the thermostat for your team. Your energy level, mood and how you react to stressful situations sets the temperature. If you walk in stressed out, then everyone will be. You walk in calm and confident, and they become so.

How we greet each other sets the tone. I also remember how welcomed and excited certain bosses were when I joined a new company. I made a point to greet people at work with enthusiasm, especially new employees on their first days. I remembered the nerves and uncomfortableness of many first days. Making a point to welcome them and ask about their story. Listening to people's stories makes them feel heard and valued.

Note to Self

**Greet people, at work and at home,
with gratitude and energy.
Be curious about their perspectives
and their stories.**

——————— ○ ———————

What I learned is that some companies will train new managers well, and others offer little support. When managers are new, they don't know what they don't know. My boss at the time taught me that my job as a manager was to make sure the people that report to me have what they need to do their job and know what their job is within the organization. It is not my job to do theirs, nor is it my responsibility to let them off the hook. I needed to do what is reasonable to help them grow, be a better employee, or learn something new. He guided me to create a team dynamic that fosters a work environment that delivers results for the company in the most efficient manner possible. I slowly learned the art of delegating tasks that can be done more efficiently by my team than by me. He showed me the importance of spending more time looking at the big picture of what my team should be delivering for the company. As a manager, you also have a boss who should be teaching and helping you. I learned to ask for help when I needed it. Just know, like me, you will make some mistakes and you will live through them. It is important, especially as a new manager, to always ask Human Resources (HR) for guidance and support on what a manager can and can't do, as it is not always obvious. I learned to do my best, be accountable, but never take my job so seriously that I forget to enjoy it. I found common sense, courtesy, and respect take care of a large aspect of every job.

Note to Self

**As a manager, I need to be the
thermostat for my team.
Set the right temperature for them to thrive.**

———— 💡 ————

Fighting corporate inertia—the established rules and ways of doing things—was the most challenging for me. Being within a business unit of a parent company that had never been required to compete in its 80-year history meant inertia was rampant. The larger the company the more the rules, paperwork, and lack of flexibility. There were rules about who qualified for certain jobs, how a candidate could be interviewed, who could be hired, and who couldn't.

I remember having to go into battle for my chosen candidate who was a single parent without a college degree. The job level required a college degree. I understood why and I understood that in most cases that made sense. However, this candidate was the best one for the job in my opinion. She was a hard worker. She was smart. She fit into the team culture. I went to HR and the president and made my case for an exception. The first conversation was a no. If they made an exception for this person, then they would be setting a precedent. I argued if they made an exception, they'd be getting the best candidate. I was frustrated. I didn't sleep that night. I couldn't let this slide. I went back the next day and fought one more time with a slightly stronger case. I got a yes! She was one of the best hires I ever made. That break also set her up for a long career in telecom.

Hiring is difficult. We try to get to know each other in an uncomfortable "grilling" interview process that does not serve either party well. We rely on assumptions and our best guesses as to the qualities that the right candidate should have. It's all we can do, but I believe hiring processes need to be open to outliers, or unicorns as I like to call them. Sometimes, employees need to be hired outside of the guidelines. Great managers can see the intensity, energy, discernment, desire, and the gratitude a candidate may have in addition to the skill sets they do or don't have. I've hired and fired many individuals over thirty years. One of my best hires was that single working mom without a college degree I had fought so hard for. One of my worst hires was an MBA grad from an elite institution. He was an academically brilliant man that could quote every business book ever written and sling a spreadsheet like no other but was so full of himself that he couldn't "see" or "listen" to anything his teammates or our customers were saying. His social skills were minimal.

There are "good" reasons for most rules and processes in big companies and our parent telecom company was no different. The challenge was they didn't understand competition and we were in an intense battle every week with our competitors. Speed was of the essence to us. We had to be innovative and creative, and we had to think outside the box. There was just a lack of understanding in the two worlds we operated.

The Internet was just beginning, and companies didn't have websites yet. Our parent company, the slow-moving behemoth telecom company, was not on the leading edge. I was head of advertising for the wireless division in the Florida region and managed our advertising agency relationships. Yes, with my former employer. We developed a "GTE Wireless HackerX" website to engage our prospects and get some media attention. I somehow sold the idea to my boss and the regional president. They didn't really understand it, but I sold it as a "test." "Just let me do it for 30 to 60 days and if it doesn't get us anything, we will shut it down."

It was thrilling and exciting—our first website page. Oops. What I didn't realize at the time we launched it and went public was that it was the global parent company GTE's first website and I had not communicated upwardly about our little project. Within 24 hours, the "suits" arrived in our little Tampa regional office demanding we shut it down. I got chewed out like I had never been chewed out before. I pleaded my case explaining to them the Internet was the future and we were going to get left behind if we didn't play. I even said something like "you should be thanking me as corporate GTE should be first" and suggested every business unit and every region should create a website. Amazing the courage you have when you are young and passionate. Needless to say, I didn't win. Shockingly, more thanks to my boss at the time who fought for me, I didn't get fired.

Note to Self

**If I am going to be bold and first,
I need to understand the rules
even if I intend to break them.
Be cautiously courageous.
Bring your boss a thank you
coffee and bagel after he saves your job.**

We were in a race every day with our competitor to get the best positioned outdoor board, the best deal on pricing with our cell phone manufacturers, and the best promo ad on our monthly wireless service. But for the most part we both did the same thing, just outsmarting each other by minimal margins of success. One significant advantage we had was our professional sports contracts. We were the official and exclusive cell phone provider for the NFL Tampa Bay Buccaneers and the NHL Tampa Bay Lightning. It was a trade only deal with both, meaning we got all the benefits and visibility of an NFL and NHL sponsorship without paying a dime. We provided free cell phone service to the management teams, coaches, and players. This was back in the day when a cell phone call was $1 a minute. We were creative in our partnerships, coming up with events for the public to meet the players and get their cell phones "tuned up." We had signage all over the stadiums and arenas. We developed great relationships with our key contacts. They became dear friends of mine, and this is where I learned relationships are everything, especially in partnerships. There is the paper contract deal and then there is the relationship. When you develop trust and give a little more when asked, you also get back a little more. The return on investment for these relations was tremendous and gave us a competitive edge in the marketplace. It also gave me some personal experiences I will never forget.

Professional sports was a man's business. When I walked into their offices, the only women I saw were receptionists, secretaries, or coordinators. Let me be crystal clear right now. I am not bringing this to your attention to bash these organizations. I loved these organizations. I am mentioning this so you can understand the courage it took to thrive in this environment. There were many intimidating elements. The physical size difference between a large group of professional male athletes and myself. The frequent cat calls, comments, and sexist looks were unwelcomed and insulting. I was there to do business, not date. And the obvious situation that would become a theme in my career, finding myself one of a few women or the only woman at the table. I spent an exorbitant amount of energy figuring out how to fit in but demand respect. It is an art, not a science. It required a delicate blend of masculine and feminine from me. I had to do my best to ignore the annoying jeers and keep walking. I befriended the wise ones and focused on the ones in charge that helped me get what we needed from the business partnership. I learned to speak their language and did my best to both show respect and demand it in return. It resulted in a great business relationship and the results were epic.

Another intimidating feature kept appearing in my business world: golf. My parents were both excellent golfers so I was hoping there might be a little DNA lotto in play. I had nothing against golf, but at the time I just didn't have time to practice or play. But it was coming up as a business skill that I needed to participate in my role. Why couldn't business be done in a ballet or a yoga class? It wasn't. It was done on a golf course. I couldn't change it. I adapted because I felt it was the only way to succeed in my role. I got the call from Fred, my dear friend managing our NHL contract. There was another charity golf tournament, all the professional sport athletes would be participating, and he wanted all the sponsor clients to participate. That would be me. Shit. The local cable station would cover it like they always did, and I reluctantly agreed.

Two weekends of lessons on the driving range was all there was time to do. Sometimes you must fake it until you make it. Fred promised me I could be with his foursome, and we would go last so I didn't have to be in the middle of NFL and NHL players on the golf course. I was the only woman again. Damn it, how does this keep happening? Anyone would have been nervous. For God's sake these were all professional athletes, they weren't even average guys. Hysterical, really. It was for charity. It was part of my job. I was dedicated to doing every aspect of my job to prove to myself and others I belonged there. I didn't want, nor did I ever ask for special treatment.

Every inch of my 5-foot, 4-inch stature walked into the event with as much fake confidence as I could muster and began mingling with these professional athletes and coaches. Just picture it for a second. Their height and their weight overpowered me by a significant margin. Many of them I had gotten to know and were amazing human beings that I admired immensely. However, there were many that were walking sexual-harassment-locker-room-poster children. Figuring out how to manage through all of it was a degree in survival.

Fred and I made it to our golf cart, and I prepared for my first shot of what I anticipated was going to be a long day. If I shanked it, Fred was a good friend, and I would be embarrassed but would survive. Then, my worst nightmare, actually something even worse than my worst nightmare, happened. As I was leaning down to put my tee in the ground, I glanced over to see the TV crew setting up about 30 feet away. The camera pointed directly at me. The look I gave Fred was something between a deer in the headlights and a terrorist ready to kill. All I could think to do was pray a desperate prayer that we are all guilty of during the moments when we find ourselves about to be humiliated.

Please Lord, if you give me nothing else, please oh please let me make a decent drive. I will go to church every Sunday. I will give to charity—wait, this is for charity. See God, I'm doing this for charity. Please just let me have a decent drive. I will be forever indebted to you for the rest of my life.

I took two or three deep breaths and desperately tried to remember everything my golf instructor had taught me in my two lessons, and I swung. Contact! Thank you, God. I looked up and there it was dead center at a respectful 100-plus yards. Two seconds later, the TV crew moved on. It was over. I did it. My shot made it on the local news that night amid all the celebrities. They showed 3 or 4 of the professional athletes that were excellent golfers and joking around entertaining the cameras, then broke to "and there was even a female in the group today raising money for the charity, Kristi Hamelryck, GTE Wireless Advertising Manager."

Note to Self

**I can do scary things.
Being a female in a man's world is hard
but I also stand out, which is a competitive edge.
Face my fears, stay calm, and carry on.**

Back in the office, I needed to figure out a way for GTE to stand out over our competition. We had both fallen into expected campaigns every few weeks. There was nothing substantially different and our numbers of new subscribers were good, but not great. I called the agency and asked for a blue ocean brainstorming session. We needed to think outside of the box. We needed to forget everything and start with a white piece of paper. No rules.

Out of this session came my favorite campaign we ever did, "Who Ordered the Phone?" We would personally deliver your cell phone in a pizza box to your home or work. The idea was to not only be focused on the phone price point and subscription promotion, but to stand out by delivering the phones to workplaces. We would deliver one phone to a workplace and simultaneously get the eyeballs of every person in that workplace. We also wanted to deliver a phone to all the on-air radio personalities and news anchors to get some free public relations airtime. It was brilliant but the logistics were close to impossible.

I presented the idea to the powers that be, and they concluded that the logistics were too risky. Not to mention our retail store managers thought it would destroy their operations. They weren't wrong. So, I went back to work and figured out a plan A, B, and C from an operational perspective. I estimated only a small percent of consumers would take us up on the offer. I negotiated with a courier service to do the actual deliveries at a decent price. This would take the pressure off our retail stores. I still wanted to build pizza box kiosks in our retail stores for the visibility, but they didn't have to do the deliveries. I had plan A, and plan B was basically a second courier service if numbers were higher than expected, and plan C was me. I was willing to be a delivery gal and I would recruit other employees and friends. It was risky, but my boss finally agreed. He did support me, but I knew if it failed, the failure would be all mine. I also held the risk that delivery costs could take us way above budget.

I didn't sleep the night before the campaign launched. I was in the office at 5 a.m. just waiting to see what was going to happen. We created a war room and watched for hourly reports of new customer sign ups and delivery requests. Day one the numbers looked good. New customer numbers were in line with our goals and only 1% were asking for deliveries. We had planned for 10%.

We waited for day two before we started the media deliveries to every top radio host. We got tremendous on-air coverage at no cost. It couldn't have gone more smoothly. By the end of the campaign, it had brought in our best new customer numbers of any previous campaign and actual delivery requests never got above 2%.

Note to Self

**Always brainstorm as if you had
a blank piece of paper and no restrictions.
Fight for ideas you believe in.
Taking risks and volunteering for
full accountability is scary,
but the rewards are empowering.**

———————— ♀ ————————

This role was perfect for me. I loved everything about it and frankly had no desire to go anywhere else. I had developed some dear friendships in the marketing department, a bonus in a job. I met my future husband during this time, bought my wedding dress in a 45-minute lunch hour and tried it on standing on top of a conference room table in the office. There is nothing more rewarding than working hard with friends and accomplishing big goals. The way we integrated our personal and professional lives made the work all that more special. Then corporate America decided to surprise me.

CAREER TWIST: FROM MARKETING GURU TO CUSTOMER SERVICE VIRGIN

Like most Fortune 50, billion-dollar corporations, the telecom giant encouraged all its "young budding executives in training" to do stints in multiple disciplines to gain broad business experience across sales, marketing, customer service, and operations. Much to my disappointment, management pulled me from my perfectly comfortable advertising role and deemed me the new leader of an inside sales team, corporate retail store, and 70-plus employee customer service center that ran twenty-four hours a day, seven days a week. My world was rocked.

I woke up the first morning of my new assignment with absolute dread. What did I know about customer service and running a sales team? I had declared management temporarily insane and prayed they would wake up with the realization of their mistake and I could go back to doing what I do best— marketing. No luck.

My new managers gave me a tour and introduced me to the five different teams, and each team member on shift. I knew nothing. I mean, I really knew nothing. There is a benefit of not knowing what you are doing. Remember that the next time you take a new job. I was completely ignorant of the normal corporate rules for customer service and sales operations teams.

I later realized this lack of knowledge was my superpower, but at the time I thought it was a detrimental weakness.

As we walked through the line of cubicles, introductions were cordial, but the individual employees seemed on guard. They were nervous about meeting the "new" boss. The majority were customer service representatives who were hourly employees. That means they clock in and clock out and are only paid for time worked. They usually have strict vacation policies like one week of vacation after six months of employment and then two weeks after a year. In a corporate organizational chart, these positions at the time were considered entry level, meaning you didn't need a lot of experience to become a customer service representative.

There I was on my first day feeling like a fish out of water, nervous and feeling completely unqualified. I had so much to learn and figure out. I just wanted to go back to creating TV and radio ads and planning all our professional sports sponsorships. I wanted to go back to my comfort zone.

Here were a few of my observations from that first day.

The individual customer service reps were treated more like cattle than humans. There were rules about when they could go to the bathroom and when they could take breaks. They had to raise their hands and the floor manager decided if it was a legit request. I asked, "Don't they know best if they have to go to the bathroom or not?" The answer I got was, "You can't trust them. They will go to the bathroom ten times to get off the phone." My response, "Seems to me if you can't trust them, you shouldn't have hired them."

I also noticed there was a huge timer keeping track of the average time of each call with customers. There were posters and notes on the wall about reducing the time of each call. Interesting, I thought to myself. In marketing, we were spending millions of dollars to get prospects and customers to talk to us and to do business with us. When I say millions of dollars, I mean a $160 million advertising budget nationally. Yet here I was in customer service, and the same company was trying to get customers off the phone. Pure insanity was my first thought. So, I asked one of the managers giving me the tour, "Why are you measuring how much time a rep spends on a customer call?"

The response, "We are a cost center, and we must be as efficient as possible. Every minute on the phone costs us money."

My third observation on this first day was the customer service reps were treated as if they were stupid. Throughout the tour, I introduced myself to each rep and chitchatted with them and my manager tour guide. In every conversation, I noticed their body language, and that during the conversation the manager acted as if the rep was not business savvy. They focused on the tactic of what to do and what not to do on a call, but there was no discussion on how our business worked and the impact a customer service rep could have on the bottom line.

So, with the realization that management was not going to pull me out of this sales and customer service role for at least a year, I chose to embrace the opportunity and figure out what success was going to look like. I took these first observations and ran with them.

First, we took away all the bathroom rules and other dehumanizing rules. We told all the employees we trusted them to make the right decision for the customer and the company. We put new goals in place that were focused on "wowing" the customer. As a team, we had to answer every call as quickly as possible, be empathetic to the customer, and resolve their issue as quickly as possible. We also wanted to take the opportunity to assess the customer account and make sure there wasn't anything they needed to adjust on their account—like a better rate plan or a new additional service that would make their experience with us more satisfying. It just made sense.

Then we took them all off the phone for a training event—it was the first time in company history. Our region was the only twenty-four hours, seven days a week customer service center in the country. We took the Midwest, Texas and California region calls after hours. My Midwest counterpart agreed to take our calls for 4 hours maximum. That was all I needed.

At this point, I had an idea but wasn't sure if it would work. I just had my intuition, and I was young, naive and had a lot of courage. My instinct told me that if I taught every customer service and sales rep how we made money and how we lost money as a company, they would make better decisions when they were speaking to the customer.

Just picture this for a moment. More than 70 customer service reps under a big white tent in an empty grass lot next to our corporate headquarters office building with a few snacks and looking at me holding a magic marker and a flip chart. Here we go!

We talked about revenue, the cost of every department including our own, and how much it costs us as a business when we lose a customer (what we call churn in the business world). We talked about how we could impact revenue per customer by selling add on services. The customer service reps were engaged, and they asked brilliant questions. It turned out they were not just human, they were smart.

I drew an organization chart. It looked like a triangle. The president was at the top of the triangle. Then the executives that report to the president were below him, and it continued down showing everyone in the organization and who they reported to in the organization. I flipped the org chart upside down so the customer service reps were on top as they were the ones closest to the customer. Then, it had me close to the bottom, my boss was below me and our president was at the bottom of the upside-down triangle.

The day before this outside team event, I swung by several of the executives' offices including my boss's and the president's and encouraged them to stop by to show their support of the great job all the customer service reps were doing. Yep, you guessed it. It was at the exact moment I wrote the president's name at the very bottom of the organization chart that they walked up. I had just stated a little verbal punch for dramatic impact of, "So you see, in my opinion, you the customer service rep are far more important than me or the president of this company." Timing is everything.

My immediate boss, who was very supportive of my crazy ideas and corporate rebel challenges, gave me a look I will never forget. I saw my career plummeting before my eyes but decided I was in too deep, so I had to finish. I continued to explain the reason why my boss and president were at the bottom. I talked about how they, as customer service reps, have far more power than we did. That as management we were here to teach and serve them, so that at that golden moment when they had our most precious assets, our customers, on the phone, they had all the tools and knowledge to make the right decision. Our customers are the reason we all get paychecks, I told them, and every customer interaction should be treated as a privilege and a moment of truth. How they treated our customers would be one of the biggest deciding factors in all of us continuing to get our paychecks in the future. We joked about the timing and that this might be my last hour as their boss. I give full credit to my boss and president at the time, they jumped in and agreed. They got it and thanked the team for all they were doing for the company.

We went on to brainstorm ideas and role played different potential conversations and scenarios with customers. They were so intelligent. They had great ideas. We did trust exercises. We looked at our risk as a department of being laid off, as it was common during this time for corporate layoffs every 2 to 3 years and they were scared. Actually, they were petrified of losing their jobs. Many were living paycheck to paycheck already and if there was ever a week without a paycheck it could put their families in a crisis mode—a basic food and shelter emergency situation. We as a team decided the best insurance against layoffs would be to become a revenue center versus a cost center. So, we set goals to soft sell add on services only if it was good for the customer. We came up with tracking and a reward program. Their excitement, their energy and their brilliance amazed me.

We had a plan. We were empowered and now we just had to execute. New posters on the wall talked about solution selling, churn reduction, and revenue goals. There were no more time clocks. The only rule was don't get off that phone until you have "WOWed" the customer. Every customer interaction was treated like a golden moment. They took care of our customers. Every stat went up and 10 months later they had sold $7.5 million in revenue to counter our $3.5 million costs as a department. They had generated enough revenue to not only cover the costs of our department but contribute a few million to the company's bottom line.

Note to Self

**If you want employees to be loyal
and act like owners of a company
then hire the right people who can be trusted,
treat them with respect, teach them the business
and trust they will make great decisions.**

Some of the employees didn't make it through the transition. We had a few exits, but the other 95% blossomed. Their body language changed. Their heads were held high. Their posture was upright. They looked management in the eyes with confidence and pride. They kept bringing new ideas to the table. They grew in their professional and personal lives. There were many who were promoted into other departments or into management. Thirty years later, it remains one of my greatest management experiences.

Many of the mentors and friendships I formed during these years are still a part of my life today. A couple went on to become brilliant CEOs, COOs, and CMOs. Others became entrepreneurs or high-ranking individual contributors. What I learned from all of them contributed significant weight to the leader I eventually became.

Note to Self

**Running a business, managing people,
and problem-solving is thrilling.
Being able to do it with people you love,
and respect is exhilarating.**

THE DOUBLE STANDARD:
THE RULES ARE DIFFERENT
FOR WOMEN

Although I observed many leadership styles in my early career years, none felt like a perfect fit for me. I couldn't miss that there were different rules for men and women. Some were innocent, almost as if they didn't realize their own bias, as these were "admirable" men who simply didn't equate their actions as breaking the rules. Other biases were conscious and deliberate.

One overt example brought this to my attention with great clarity. A "no gift" policy from vendors is a common rule in companies. I was aware of the gift policy but had witnessed and even organized many sporting events for our executives that included valued gifts well over the $25 maximum value limit. With so many professional sports marketing sponsorships, we were routinely invited to all-expenses-paid golf tournament weekends. Many times, executives would participate and even include their wives along for the "free" weekend. It was a very normal part of our business. During this same time, I went to New York for a weekend celebration with four work girlfriends. The trip had multiple purposes from my friend's family visits, to just a plain girls' weekend, and to celebrate my engagement. Two of the girls worked at the agency, which was one of our vendors, and two of us worked for the telecom company. To my surprise, once we got to New York they treated me to a few dinners and Broadway shows. It was not planned and there was a blurry line between work and friendship. I really didn't think much of it.

A few weeks later I was called into the president's office with a Human Resource representative present. They informed me they had heard about the trip, and it broke the rule of gift giving from a vendor. They asked details and I told them everything I could remember and took full responsibility explaining it was very innocent. One thing I have never faltered on in my entire career is accountability. There is no one, and I mean no one, that is harder on myself than me. I will always step up and own my mistakes and take full accountability. This was no different. I offered to pay back anything that needed to be paid back as it was truly innocent. They explained to me they would discuss it and figure out the consequences. As I was walking out of the office, it occurred to me that this situation was no different than the weekend golf trips for our executives where wives were included. So, I turned back to them and said, "I regret that I broke a rule that I truly never intentionally meant to break, and I hate that this has made us all realize we have to pay back all the golf tournament weekends and free golf attire. It is going to be hard to even figure out the dollar amount for all those weekends as it must be thousands of dollars. Let me know how far back we need to go to collect all the hundreds of gifted golf tournament weekends our executives have taken over the past many years."

I never heard another word about it. Rules are rules and should be respected, but you can't have one rule for men, golf, and wives and another rule for women, dinner, and Broadway. Some of the biases were conscious and misogynistic but many were unconscious and innocent. Someone had to bring it to their attention, a burden I would later grow weary of, but I continued being a voice of reason. I wasn't asking for special treatment, I was asking for equal treatment, nothing more.

Those who think it is no big deal, most likely fall in a category of those who the biases favor. They wouldn't see the need to change things. I never set out to be a fighter for equality, I just found myself in situation after situation that needed awareness and change. But I wanted to do it in a way that could bring people along with me, not create animosity. Being careful how you say things, to whom you say things, and presenting alternatives so as not to alienate the ones that have the power to make the changes was challenging. In some cases, it was as simple as bringing it to their attention, in other cases it had to be their idea. The delicate balance of being a changemaker, dancing around egos, and getting the result was a dance. I knew how to dance.

Note to Self

**Speaking up is not something I want to do
but feels like something I must do.
It is not just a choice but a responsibility to make things
more equitable for me and those that follow.**

THE DECISION TO GET MARRIED: WITNESSING WRONG ASSUMPTIONS

As a woman focused on her career, getting married and having kids was a big decision for me. Everything I had observed to that point told me it would negatively impact my career trajectory. When I met my husband, I knew he was the one after the first date, but we both agreed to date for five years before getting married because of our careers. He was in the middle of raising money and building two Fat Tuesday bars and restaurants. I was signing up for any career opportunity that presented itself which usually meant moving every two years. Many people in our immediate circle gave him a hard time, assuming he was the one delaying, another society bias.

My husband and I have been and continue to be each other's greatest life lessons and teachers. Our differences have helped both of us be more accepting and better human beings. We challenge each other's thinking, and for the most part, respectfully agree to disagree on what we can't find common ground on, but we have enough common ground to have a strong foundation. When we cut through all the nonsense and really talk things out, we usually find we are more similar than different. I didn't want someone exactly like me. I wanted someone good at things I wasn't and who challenged me. He is an engineer, financier, and an academically intelligent, introverted human. I am a creative, marketing, operations, intelligent, extroverted human. We view problems and the world differently at first blush, but at our deepest levels we align in that magical middle. There it is again: differences are a good thing.

I had a surprising identity crisis when I got married. I had so much trouble giving up my maiden name. It was who I was for 26 years. I had also taken such pride in the uniqueness of my name—Hamelryck. There were only nine of us in America at the time. It always triggered a conversation about my blended heritage as no one had heard of it or could spell it. No offense to my husband but "Turner" was a common name. It was like Smith. I just couldn't see myself with a common American name. Also, I had worked extremely hard building a business network of contacts across the country. I knew most job opportunities come from those who you have worked with in the past. How would they find me if my name changed? How would people I grew up with find me? It felt like Kristi Hamelryck, someone I knew and trusted, was being replaced by Kristi Turner, someone I didn't know. It was a real struggle for me. I held on to my maiden name for a couple of years at work. I went by Kristi Hamelryck-Turner, but the length was ridiculous, and I eventually just simplified. I wish I would have adopted the Spanish tradition of keeping your mother's maiden name and your father's surname. It makes so much sense to me. As we are each 50/50 of our father and mother. It seems so much more respectful to your heritage on both sides.

Note to Self

Our differences are a good thing.
My name is part of my identity.
Changing it is a big deal.

———— ○ ————

I was so glad we got married in our late 20s and early 30s. We both entered the marriage knowing who we were as individuals.

I was extremely grateful I had time to make some critical life decisions and experiences before I got married. Who I chose to marry looked very different from those I chose to date when I was younger. I loved the experience of buying a condo on my own and making career decisions on my own before getting married.

Then, there was the monumental decision to have kids. So many working females struggle with this one as our "prime" time to physically have kids is usually at our "prime" time in career progression. All the things I had heard and observed in corporate culture battled in my mind. "You have to choose family or career." *What?* I loathed this phrase. What a cop out. It was always targeted at women. It was admirable for a man to have a career and be a father, but a woman needed to choose between the two.

I had witnessed three executives deciding the fate of several next generation employees. One candidate in the discussion was a man. The executives commented that he and his wife had just had a baby, so he "was ready" for a promotion as he was providing for a family now. The group discussed several other individuals, and their skill sets and whether they were ready or not. Then they discussed a female individual that they thought was incredibly talented, and a go-getter, but she had just gotten married and was probably going to have kids soon, so she likely didn't want the pressure of a promotion. *Are you kidding me?* They decided her fate based on assumptions about her personal life. They likely thought they were being kind and fair. It was horrifying to witness. It is so sad to think about all the "what ifs" for all the women. Careers were shut down or limited by a few decision-makers that did not even give the women a chance to make their own decisions.

It was difficult to endure all I had witnessed, and still not believe if I had kids my career was going to stall or plummet. The idea that I had to choose was ludicrous to me. The idea that if I worked, I would be less as a mother and if I chose not to work, I was a better mother didn't make sense to me, either. The idea that men did not have the same responsibility to parent children was absurd. Luckily, there were a few examples around me that gave me some hope that it could be done well. It was the first time I had read the infamous quote, "The tyranny of OR versus the genius of AND." I was going to choose the genius of AND.

My husband and I talked, delayed a little, and then realized like everyone else you are never really ready, so you just do it. There were a few adventurous bucket list items I chose to knock off before pregnancy—skydiving and hang-gliding. I kept thinking everything was going to change when I had kids. I was not going to be a risk taker. I would never get another promotion. I wouldn't have time to work out. I was wrong about it all except the fact that everything was going to change. That change just happened to be in a good way.

I was a cautious adventurer, meaning I pushed myself to do daredevil adventures once or maybe twice. Yet I also craved security and safety. It was another dichotomy in me. The adrenaline adventures remind me I am brave and alive and give me more confidence in the aftermath of facing something I fear. But rest assured, I am not fearless. The whole point is I am facing something I fear, not learning to be fearless. Adventures gave me a different perspective on life and the world. When looking down from 7000 feet in the air, the hustle and bustle looked like an ant farm. It was serene and calm. I was one tiny human in this big world and from that perspective it felt like nature was a bigger component than humans. It made me rethink, especially at a point when I was bringing another human into this world. I found that quietness high above the chaos reminded me of the importance of stillness between the adrenaline and the relief.

Similarly, in the work environment, the ebbs and flows of adrenaline deadlines and intense projects were exhilarating, but we all needed a pause afterwards to regroup and recover. Too much adrenaline becomes overwhelming for our nervous system and too much stillness creates boredom. Finding the balance between the two is the magic in the middle. Having kids was going to give me another dynamic in my life to intertwine with all the rest. More than anything else, they were going to give me a whole new perspective.

Note to Self

The extremes are necessary for me, but valuing the stillness in the middle is important. Seeing the big picture gives me a different perspective.

HOW BEING A PARENT
MADE ME A BETTER
BUSINESS LEADER AND HUMAN

Being a mother has been my greatest joy. Having children made me a better manager of people. Having children made me a better person. I learned that you don't know how you will feel until you are in the moment, nor would all those that knew me at the time have ever predicted what I felt when that firstborn showed up. I chose to keep my pregnancy private for five months as I was up for a potential promotion and feared my career would stall. During my pregnancy, one of the executives approached me about a phenomenal opportunity in Puerto Rico. Even though PR was part of the US, it was treated as an international assignment. I had wanted to do an international assignment for years. This was my chance, but I was pregnant. I wasn't ready yet to give up the idea. So, silence was just buying me time to think through it all. It was a golden opportunity that would include a significant increase in salary with all housing and living expenses paid. I wrestled with the decision for days. I couldn't have a baby in Puerto Rico. I didn't know one person in Puerto Rico at the time. I knew my husband would support me if I absolutely wanted to do it, but everything about it was unrealistic. I reluctantly declined the opportunity with some other excuse as it couldn't be because I was pregnant.

I worked through my due date. It was Friday the 25th and I left work at 5:30 p.m. baffled that my baby did not come on the exact due date. I had no control. What a great lesson! I was working on a special project assignment for the president at the time and I had planned everything and tied it all nice and neat with a bow so the project would not skip a beat while I was on maternity leave. I went home and did squats, walked, lifted weights, and stretched. I ate eggplant parmesan and followed the instructions of any other old wives' tale I'd heard to induce labor. Yes, I lifted weights and did cardio until the day she was born. I wore heart rate monitors and just took everything down 20%. Finally, Sunday morning, on the 27th, baby Lexie arrived.

The feelings that flooded my mind, body, and soul in that moment that I became a parent were just indescribable. It was transformational and transcendental at the same time. Granted, it is different for everyone. For me, it was this love that had an intensity that I had never felt before. I couldn't leave her side. I didn't even let them take her to the nursery. I wanted her right there by my bed. I wanted my husband there. I just couldn't stop staring at her. This life that we were now responsible for needed something every minute of a 24-hour day or maybe every few hours of a 24-hour day. It just felt like minutes as we had to make sure she was breathing while she slept. It was overwhelming but also felt so natural.

She was ours and she seemed perfect. I chose a natural birth as I already had one foot in the homeopathy world and felt if I could, I would. So, I did. Hard? Hmm, yes. Any regrets? Absolutely none. My body had a history of not dealing with pain medication well, so I was concerned. I was also more afraid of an epidural in my spine than I was of the pain of childbirth. All I could think of was paralysis. My labor was 8 to 9 hours, and it was extreme pain, but bearable. I thought once or twice about giving in, but I somehow knew I could do it. My husband and my doula were the only ones with me, and they both helped me tremendously. The experience of giving birth is miraculous and I think unique for every woman and for each birth. It is magical, euphoric, painful, and spiritual. I was fully present for all of it. I was so thankful I was one of the lucky ones without complications.

That was the first visible criticism I noticed about choosing to do healthcare differently than the majority. The nurses at the hospital made it very clear they disagreed with my choice. I was somewhat naive before this. I never thought anyone would care what I chose for myself. The only pain it caused was for me. I was not asking anything extra of them. Why should they care? I was so wrong. The judgment was intense, and the feelings were made very clear by every single nurse. They offered minimal support as I guess it was their way of punishing me. Little did I know that was just the beginning of the judgment. If you don't do what the majority does, then you "pay" for it in some form or another.

Note to Self

**Choosing to go down the path less followed,
the minority versus the majority,
can feel uncomfortable and lonely.
You need courage, stamina, and a support system
as you will receive criticism and judgment.**

What I thought before the birth of my first child and what I thought after surprised us all. My priorities shifted in an instant. Ms. Overachieving Workingwoman wanted to stay home forever and never leave the house. I just wanted to be with my daughter. Time with her became non-negotiable.

Sometimes what we want isn't what we get. The reality was even though I wanted to stay home longer than my 12-week maternity leave, at the time we couldn't financially swing it. Hence, I had to go back to work. My company had just opened a corporate sponsored daycare across the street from my office. It was partially subsidized, and both were 10 minutes from my house. I had the best setup possible, but it still was too much for me to be away from her from 8 a.m. to 5 p.m. I negotiated with my boss to work from home in the late afternoons. It was about as good as it gets considering at the time working from home was neither popular nor accepted.

I got joy from work, and I got joy from being a mom. For me, it was just about getting creative with my schedule and doing it differently. We woke up, breastfed, showered, packed lunches, and headed into work. I dropped her off at 8 a.m., went to meetings, pumped at 11 a.m. in a closet at work, ran across the street to visit during lunch hour and back to meetings. I usually picked her up around 2 p.m., came home and put her down for her three-hour nap and then got back to work. We were home and playing in the evening hours until she went to bed around 7:30 p.m. and I was back to work. My job did not suffer at all. In fact, I believe I gave more in gratitude to my boss and my company. I was so grateful for the daycare at work, and the afternoons to work from home that I gave them more of me.

Note to Self

Don't try to predict how you feel in the future.
You don't know until you are there.
Give yourself permission to change your mind.
Great bosses who give a little actually get more in return.

From both the employee and the business bottom line perspective, maternity/paternity leave, healthcare, and daycare benefits are essential to career decisions, equality, and employee retention. They have an impact on employees' ability to excel at their job. These benefits are incredibly expensive to a company's bottom line. Healthcare costs especially have skyrocketed over the years. However, the cost of attracting and retaining talented employees tends to be more costly.

Finding the right balance of expense and benefit is a constant leadership struggle. As an employee with a growing family, the importance of such benefits became essential to my career decisions going forward. I admired companies who were expanding maternity leave to paternity leave, encouraging a better balance of parenting between males and females.

A dear friend of mine did a brilliant move with his newborns. Given the physical demands having a baby placed on his wife, it was logical she take traditional maternity leave at time of birth. She took 12 weeks maternity leave from the birth date, and he took the next 12 weeks paternity leave. It gave him the gift of bonding with his child and figuring out creative solutions that were different from his wife's. It helped her have peace of mind that her precious baby was with his father and not have to adjust back to work with the challenge of navigating daycare all at the same time. It gave her the gift of focus. That is what equality looks like.

My brother-in-law also had this opportunity more by accident than by plan, but it created a bond with his two young daughters that most dads never have the opportunity to create. They were moving states and my sister who was a nurse started work immediately and his work did not start for a few months. They had just had their second child. He spent a few months as a stay-at-home dad. His problem-solving was the opposite of hers and brilliant I must say. My niece loved yogurt but made a mess. He quickly took a fat straw, popped it in the top with the tin foil intact and put a rubber band around it. It was so much easier for their toddler and no mess. Brilliant.

Note to Self

**Men and women are opposite in so many ways.
They approach problem solving from opposite directions.
Both can be brilliant.
Different solutions to the same problem are possible.**

Until companies started offering paternity leave, it wasn't even an option for fathers. Does policy drive change or does demand drive policy? Both. There has been progress but not enough. There are still far too many news stories positioning daycare as a female issue. It is a parent issue and both parents need to demand better policies. The more employees and leaders that demand better paternity leave and encourage parents to take paternity leave, the better balance of life-work for all. And I believe the better chance a company has to retain talent.

My focus on health continued to increase as well after having my first child as I saw the connection more clearly between mental health, sick days, and the ability to do my job. I had watched my dad's deteriorating health and the decline in his ability to do his job. As a manager, I experienced the negative impact of employees calling in sick or dealing with life struggles that made their performance decline. When employees call in sick in most cases their workload falls on the manager or other team members. Health issues cost both the employee and the company time, money, and productivity. It is both a business problem and a personal problem. It has driven many companies to promote health initiatives to encourage employees to adopt healthier lifestyles. Personally, when you deal with health issues for yourself or for a family member, it becomes your number one focus and everything else in your life takes a backseat. My special interest in health kept increasing as I saw the broader negative implications.

As a new parent there was more to juggle and more stress on my mental and physical health. Like the ballet days, there were no sick days allowed as a parent. Staying healthy was essential to taking care of my child, my ability to do my job and handle stress. I continued studying and experimenting with different stress techniques, yoga, strength training, chiropractic, and healthy food as medicine. It wasn't about me anymore. It was about my child. I was also looking for a different type of work culture than the traditional in-office mandate.

Note to Self

Staying healthy is more important than ever for me, my job, and my kids.

———— 💡 ————

When Lexie was about 9 months old, my wonderful boss left the company for another opportunity. He asked me to take on his role as Acting VP of Marketing. I was honored and took it willingly knowing it was most likely temporary. We were in the middle of the largest telecom merger in history. GTE and Bell Atlantic were becoming Verizon. Everything would shift, hence the "acting" versus permanent opportunity. Our president at the time asked me what I wanted. The position I was in would be based in New Jersey at the new headquarters. We were happy in Atlanta and had no desire to move to Jersey, so I asked for a severance package. I also had an amazing opportunity that offered a more desirable home/work life balance and allowed me to continue a great career.

Two former telecom executive women had left the traditional corporate world to create a consulting company. They both were very successful leaders, had young kids and wanted a better home/work lifestyle. It was my first experience seeing successful women venture into the entrepreneurial world and succeed. It was so refreshing. At the time, it was a very forward-thinking model. They had their consulting company and then recruited many former telecom experts to work as subcontractors under their direct contracts with several large global telecom companies. All of us as individuals formed our own consulting companies, most through LLCs or S corps. The opportunity allowed me to work on important strategic telecom industry projects, choose my hours from part-time to over-time, and work from home. Given that my heart and soul were literally wrapped around my daughter, it was an unbelievable opportunity at a perfect time in my life. I am forever grateful to these two women for having the courage to build a different business model that created a new kind of work environment.

Note to Self

**Sometimes the quicker way to change things
is to create a new reality
instead of fighting to change the old reality.**

I was able to continue building my resume working on projects with top telecom companies like AT&T, Ericsson, T-Mobile, and Comcast, yet be the one greeting my daughter as she woke up from her afternoon nap. It was this working mom's dream. The consulting projects were strategic, interesting, and complex business challenges. It was during the time that Apple and Google were disrupting the telecom world. We were researching this new world of "content" and streaming and how it might change multiple industries. The power was shifting from service providers to hardware manufacturers and content providers. The market share leaders that were giants just years before were falling and some were becoming obsolete. Apple and Google were redefining the rules and the telecom giants weren't shifting quickly enough. To be in the middle of the strategic discussions and watch the transition in the telecom wireless world from the 1990s to 2005 was thrilling. I loved every minute of predicting the future and strategizing potential market shifts and outcomes. Even though I wanted more flexibility in my work life, I didn't want less intellectually challenging work. If more companies could realize the value of offering hybrid work models, I think they would see the benefit of retaining top talent.

During this rewarding career time, my husband and I were also contemplating having baby number two. Lexie was two years old, and we didn't want our kids too many years apart. I knew I wanted a second child, but I didn't feel ready. Lexie was a handful. Her nickname at daycare was "mighty mouse" and "energizer bunny." From the time she woke up until the time she went to sleep, she literally never stopped. She was walking at 9 months and running at 9 months and one day. She had an intense personality and was one of the happiest outgoing toddlers you would ever meet. She had wild blonde curly hair and a dynamic personality to go with it. She was fearless to a point of concern. She would run and jump in a pool while looking backwards. She never met a stranger. As exhausting as chasing her all day was her pure joy for life gave me so much energy. Just being around her made me smile all the time. My slight hesitation to have number two was simply fear of juggling two wild ones and having the capacity to love them both. Of course, what I discovered is you don't divide your love between multiple kids, your ability to love just expands. Isn't it amazing how much a heart can hold.

My second pregnancy was like my first. I was healthy and had no major complications except gestational diabetes. I was able to control that with my healthy diet that I was already following. The most difficult thing in my second pregnancy was there was absolutely no rest time. I was in a slow jog chasing Lexie the entire pregnancy.

What was different was we chose to not find out the gender ahead of time for our second. So much of what I had for Lexie was non-gendered and neutral, as I wasn't a pink princess kind of mom. So, my pre-planning personality felt more at ease. I thought this might be our last, so I wanted to experience what it felt like to not know. One of the few things left in life that is God's surprise.

The birth was a double surprise, it was a boy and he arrived three weeks early. How does the saying go, "If you want to make God laugh, just show him your plans." I chose to do an all-natural birth again and had a similar experience with the medical staff. If eyes could speak, it was obvious, they disapproved. Baby Jack came out seemingly healthy according to Western medicine assessments. We were thrilled and made our way home as quickly as possible to settle into our new life as a family of four.

The differences between my first and second child were evident from the beginning. It wasn't just male versus female, but it was their personalities and polar opposite infancy experience. Jack was glued to me from day one. He was colicky and only slept a couple of hours. He had repetitive ear infections and cold symptoms. You could tell he was uncomfortable. My pediatrician's only solution was ongoing antibiotics and ear tube surgery. I kept voicing my concerns that there must be a root cause to his colic behavior. Was he allergic to something? I voiced my discomfort with repetitive antibiotics, and just got the brush off. My pediatrician kept saying, "Hang in there, he will grow out of it." Every cell in my body knew that was wrong.

I researched colic babies relentlessly trying to figure out other options. I had been getting chiropractic care since my first pregnancy and both of my kids had been getting adjustments since they were a week old. My chiropractor had become a dear friend. She encouraged me to see a naturopath since I was dissatisfied with my pediatrician's advice. I had experience with some alternative Eastern medicine, but I had no idea what a naturopath was at this time. I was sleep deprived, desperate, and determined to find something to give my baby boy some relief. I had done everything my pediatrician had recommended and he wasn't any better. Ear tube surgery was a nightmare as Jack came out of surgery with a negative reaction to the anesthesia screaming bloody murder and flailing his arms and legs. It didn't feel right.

All I knew going into our first naturopath appointment was that naturopathy focused on root causes and non-invasive, more natural treatments versus symptom-focused pharma remedies. She tested Jack using muscle response testing which as a mother I fell in love with as it was noninvasive. No needles, no scratches, and no harm to my 10-month-old baby. She explained that Jack was sensitive to multiple foods and environmental items. She recommended using a technique called Nambudripad's Allergy Elimination Technique (NAET) which would eliminate the sensitivities one by one. Insurance wouldn't cover it and only one treatment could be done at a time, so it would take multiple visits.

I was married to a Georgia Tech engineer who saw the world in black and white and like most of us rightfully believed we should follow doctors' advice. Here is how I positioned it. We had given our pediatrician 10 months and $2500 which was just meeting the insurance deductible. With insurance and the surgery, we had really given her $10,000 and our son was no better. I said I am going to give the naturopath 10 months and $2500 before I judge if her methods were working or not. I thought that was fair and logical. He agreed.

It only took five weeks and $200 before we knew it was working. After the first five allergy elimination techniques, Jack's dark circles and pale skin transformed. He had color and looked healthier. He was smiling more. He went from waking up every 1 to 2 hours at night to sleeping 12 solid hours without waking up. He transitioned from 45-minute naps during the day to 3 to 4 hour naps a day. I had to wake him up at 5 p.m. to eat dinner and play, then turn around and put him back to sleep at 7:30 p.m. It was like he was catching up on sleep after 10 months of sleep deprivation. He was no longer clinging to me. It was miraculous. We continued the treatments and I even started doing NAET treatments for myself and Lexie. Everything the naturopath said and did made perfect sense and worked better than anything else I had ever tried.

I could write an entire book on the benefits of naturopathic and alternative medicine. For now, I will just say, she became our family doctor of choice, and my family of four has gone to her for over 20 years. I am a strong believer in alternative Eastern medicine including naturopathy, chiropractic, acupuncture, energy medicine, detox therapy, exercise, nutrition, spiritual emotional release, herbs, essential oils, sage, cold therapy, saunas and so much more. My son has been one of the healthiest kids I know since he was 11 months old. He went from antibiotics every 4 to 5 weeks to not needing an antibiotic for the next 19 years. I believe the body continues to give us messages that something is wrong. It is like a check engine light, and it starts soft and gets louder and more severe until you address it. Unfortunately, we tend to ignore the signals or numb the symptoms.

It's been great to witness many Eastern medicine techniques being more widely accepted, but unfortunately many are still not covered by insurance, making them unattainable for a lot of the population. Maybe one day we will see the growth of wellness centers, where Eastern and Western practitioners work together sharing their genius with each other and insurance will cover what is best for each individual patient. Both have something to offer. The sick care model is not working well for keeping us healthy and productive. There are multiple ways to solve problems. If only collaboration and wellness could become the priority, and biases could be dropped. Again, it is "not the tyranny of OR but the genius of AND."

Note to Self

**There are always multiple solutions to one problem.
Explore all options.
Alternative medicine has produced
amazing results for many.
Western medicine can be very valuable.
Our healthcare system is broken.
There are biases and controls in our current
healthcare system that do not serve our health.**

Wellness is important to individuals, families, and companies. If we could get it right, there are tremendous benefits to our stress levels, productivity outputs, and financial situations. More important than all of that, we tend to be happier when we are healthier. As we say in business, happy employees = happy customers = happy bottom line.

This season of gaining significant career experience and having two children under the age of 4 was a roller coaster ride with much gratitude and joy. Having my own consulting company and being an entrepreneur was a new experience with inverse advantages and disadvantages compared to the corporate world. In the corporate world there are health benefits, insurance, 401Ks, stock purchase options, discounted daycare and so many other fringe benefits. There is also inefficiency, politics, and bureaucracy. As an entrepreneur, one must sell, deliver, and figure out the right tax strategies, self-employment insurance options, and alternative retirement plans. Entrepreneurs must wear all the hats. They are their own billing department and their own IT department. There is more flexibility, freedom, and zero bureaucracy. Understanding the ins and outs of a medium-sized advertising agency, a Fortune 50-billion-dollar telecom company and a small entrepreneurial consulting company made me appreciate all aspects of business. It opened my perspective to the many different options of earning a living, all with very different pros and cons. It also gave me the confidence that I could be successful and happy in any size company and dynamic. There was a freedom in that confidence. I knew no matter what I decided to do or needed to do in the future, I had choices and options.

I think the more diverse experiences and work environments in the beginning of a career can yield a sort of superpower. Many choose to stay in one type of business for most of their careers and although I agree that kind of focus can have its benefits, the negative is getting stuck in the inertia of one way of doing things. It is more about finding what works for you in different seasons. Reevaluating what you need from work and what you don't want from your work in any particular season is a powerful exercise. Anything is "figureoutable." Trust yourself and be creative.

The positive influence my kids had on my work was the surprise of the century. I focused more and produced faster. I had more compassion and patience with coworkers and employees. Having a daughter and a son helped me understand the female-male dynamic at work better. My kids made me smile and laugh every single day, which made me a happier person at home and work.

One of my favorite things about the infant-to-toddler stage was seeing the world through their eyes. Jack was so observant, precise, and asked a million questions a day. My mother-son relationship was different from my mother-daughter relationship. Having a son helped me understand my husband more. There were so many unexpected bonuses of having kids. Each child gave me something unique. They were both just fascinating little humans.

Their curiosity and questions about everything made me rethink how I saw the world. Their excitement to watch bugs was contagious. I had to really think as they asked me all their "why" questions. Why did it rain? Why do ants crawl and not talk? Why does the moon go away when the sun shows up? Why does a tree have limbs? The questions were endless and so intuitive. It made me ask more questions in my work environment. Why do we do things that way? Is there a better way?

It was my kids that taught me to adopt two questions in my work environment that would turn out to drive innovation and efficiency in multiple businesses in the future: "Why?" and "What if?"

Note to Self

Asking why and what if leads to new ideas, joyful moments, and opportunities. Adopting a kid's curiosity leads to innovation in the work environment.

Every young working woman I have had the honor to mentor asks me one question, "How did you have kids and keep climbing the corporate ladder?" I never hesitate to answer, "Having kids made me a better business leader and a more whole human being. It was the best decision I ever made for my career." If I hadn't had kids, I would have missed so much love, joy, and laughter. I think mothering gave me more balance to have something I cared about more than my career to focus on. The irony is that everybody focuses on the difficulty of balancing home life and work life, but I credit my kids for giving me a better balance. Yes, being a parent is exhausting. There are no breaks and most of us are not good at asking for help. The daily duties and schedules are overwhelming and endless. Children also humble you, love you, and remind you what is truly important every day. The contrast between work and home gave me a better perspective of life.

The kids knew they were my priority. We had fun and a pretty good healthy lifestyle, between chiropractic, naturopathy, eating healthily, and exercising. We did it all. Thanks to our naturopath more than anything, my kids were really healthy. They might get a cold or a virus once a year but were over it quickly. They had very few sick days so I would encourage them to take a mental health day occasionally. Even though they had "permission" to take one, they very rarely did. Was that because I didn't? Was I modeling the right behavior for them? You know the old saying, "Do as I say, not as I do." Looking back now, I realize I modeled how to do it all, but I didn't model how to rest. I also didn't model how to ask for help or divide child rearing responsibilities evenly. Some of that was my fault. I wanted control of how things were done with the kids, and I didn't know how to ask for help.

When both spouses work, the household and child responsibilities MUST be divided as evenly as possible. Literally, write down all the list of responsibilities and I mean everything. Figure out how to divide them as evenly as possible between the two of you. A relationship will be strained if it is unfairly balanced for years. It takes so much effort and so much ongoing communication that most couples give up or fall into their corners and accept that it is what it is. It creates resentment. You can't ever get those years back. It is important that kids get time and nurturing from both parents, not one parent. I didn't do this well and I paid a heavy price of exhaustion for many years. It's not healthy, and more importantly, it is not fair. There are so many things in life that are unfair that we can't control. This is one of those things I could have done better. As I learned I am 100% responsible for 50% of all my relationships.

Note to Self

I am 100% responsible for 50% of all my relationships.
What I bring to the relationship is on me.
I need to communicate my needs.
I need to ask for help and be able to receive help.

What I didn't do is release control or ask for help. I would get angry and then get silent. I would let resentment build up and that was all on me. As I've shared with friends over the years, I came to realize this little routine was not unique to us. One partner is proactive, and the other reactive. One partner sees things that need to get done and proactively does them. One partner wants things done a certain way and wants control. The other partner steps back and lets the other one do most of the tasks. Here is the odd part that almost makes me laugh it is so ridiculous. The partner that does most of the work quietly starts building resentment for having to do it all. They feel righteous in their opinion as anyone from the outside would see them doing most of the work. Simultaneously, the other partner doing less household work and child tasks is building resentment as the exhausted partner is giving all their attention to the children, feeling ignored. They also feel righteous that they are being neglected.

The irony is the only fix for the exhausted partner is to release control of certain tasks and the other partner to get involved and start doing. Funny enough that rarely happens. The martyr keeps being the martyr and the parent doing less tasks keeps doing less out of spite. Resentment builds and communication lessens. Oh, the irony! Then the blowup happens, and both are appalled at the other's perspective. They just can't believe it. They both feel so "right" in their feelings. Couples explore therapy, divorce, or most of the time it is just easier to keep on going in their misery. As humans, we tend to think repeating the same old patterns is the easier path, but it is just continuing the dysfunctional cycle. Change is difficult and seeing another person's perspective is even more difficult, yet that is exactly where the solution is for a healthier happier life for both partners. If you are overburdened at home, it usually negatively impacts your success at work. If you are overburdened at work, it negatively impacts your home life.

In my work world, every time I witnessed an otherwise solid performing employee suddenly have uncharacteristic issues at work, I could surmise they were having struggles in their personal life. It would suddenly come out they were in the middle of a divorce or dealing with a health crisis or an addiction. Stress from one, impacts the other. Becoming more self-aware, learning to communicate better, and adopting stress-reducing techniques help in both our personal and professional lives.

Note to Self

**I need to learn to communicate.
I need to understand others' perspectives.
I need to stop trying to do it all.
I only know how to do it all.**

It was a stranger's advice that shocked me into changing a few things that I didn't even realize I needed to change at the time. I was sitting in my chiropractor's waiting room with my two young children as a stranger began to make conversation. I was exhausted and not in the mood for small talk, but he was persistent. He asked me how old my children were, and what I did for a living. So, I politely and precisely answered the questions with my head down and avoided eye contact in hopes the conversation may end.

"So, you are a mother and a consultant in the corporate world?" he continued.

"Yes, I am," I said.

"What do you do to nourish yourself?" he asked next.

"I work out regularly. I am a yoga teacher and a certified personal trainer," I answered.

"So, you're a parent, a consultant, a yoga teacher, and a personal trainer? You seem to lead or teach in all aspects of your life. Do you ever give yourself the gift of being a student?" he asked.

I looked up to meet his eyes for the first time and asked, "What do you mean?"

"In life, we all need to find a balance. At any age we need to be both a student and a teacher. Always give yourself the gift of being a student in some aspect of your life. You don't have to always be the teacher."

After this profound statement he got up and walked out of the office. I thought it was one of the best insights anyone had ever shared with me. It made so much sense. I shifted a few things in my life after this interaction. The next morning, I resigned as a yoga teacher. The thing I enjoyed the most, I vowed to never teach again. I wanted to be a lifelong student of yoga. I stopped training other people as a personal trainer and just used the knowledge for myself.

Note to Self

**Make sure you are a student in some aspect of your life
to nourish your soul and to learn.
Don't try to lead in everything you do.**

I needed a better balance between leading and learning, giving, and receiving. Just shifting in two areas helped me tremendously. I could go to yoga class and stand in the back and just practice without thinking, planning, or being noticed. It was a micro shift that had a macro impact.

However, I was still a classic overachiever and sometimes even when we know better, we don't always do better. I had made some good adjustments in certain areas, and I was aware of the need to ask for help but not really applying the tactics of asking for help. I was still in some ways following my martyr syndrome of "doing it all." Then a leadership opportunity in corporate America came into my life. More responsibility. More pressure. More juggling. Sounds great. Brilliant.

SEASON THREE:

THE LEADERSHIP YEARS:
VIEW FROM THE TOP, TEAM DYNAMICS,
AND RAISING THE NEXT GENERATION

BEING A NEWBIE: FINDING MY FOOTING, LEARNING THE ROPES

The leadership years, reporting directly to the CEO, began when I least expected. My kids were 5 and 2 years old and I was in my early 30s. I felt very challenged, balanced, and satisfied working as a consultant with a stellar group of individuals on truly interesting industry-impacting projects. Daily life was exhausting yet exhilarating. I ran on adrenaline as most parents of young children do. I think we block out the exhaustion when we are in the middle of it. I didn't see it then. Part of us knows there is no other option, or at least we tell ourselves that. In the absence of options, we keep on keeping on. Adrenaline gets us through the "little sleep all activity" years. There is also a strength that we pull from as a parent. These helpless little humans depend on us for their basic daily needs. We don't even think about it. We just do it.

In between the exhaustion were the smiles, cuddles, and giggles that filled my soul. Laughter was what gave me energy during the early parenting years. Their energy and joy were contagious. This is the weird dynamic with kids. They are the reason we are exhausted, but they are also the ones that give us the energy to get through the exhaustion.

In the middle of it all, a career opportunity of a lifetime that I wasn't looking for in the least came along. One of my former bosses introduced me to an investor who was looking for a marketing executive for his financial technology start-up. The investor was a legend, with a stellar reputation, and a long history of business successes. I had no desire to go back to a long daily commute and office environment. I entered the interview process with a completely different dynamic than previous interviews given I was happy as a consultant. I wasn't desperate to win the job. I felt an incredible freedom through the process. I realized that when you are willing to walk away from any negotiation— buying a business, asking for a pay raise, or with a 3-year-old toddler—you bring a more confident and authentic energy to the table. It also reiterated something else I was slowly witnessing. The most successful negotiations are a win-win for both parties, not a win-lose. A "deal" where one party loses, and the other party wins may appear to be a short-term triumph but rarely ever is successful in the long-term.

Note to Self

**Be willing to walk away from a
negotiation before you ever begin.
If you are desperate,
you will end up with the sour end of the deal.**

This venture investor was known for investing capital into technology start-ups and creating multi-million and even billion-dollar business deals. More importantly, he had a reputation for doing business with integrity, respect, and even a handshake. He was known to be fair. He had been described to me as the "Warren Buffett of the South."

We first met in his small hometown office which I thought was understated for someone with his business success record.

Within the first ten minutes of meeting him, it all made sense. He was brilliant, warm, welcoming, humble, and kind. He asked me about where I was from and about my family. We talked about our common passion for customers and employees. He explained his family's 100-year value system. He was such a breath of fresh air. He was a wildly successful businessman that was down to earth, cared about individuals' personal stories, and had a true passion for entrepreneurs.

Being honest to a fault, at the end of our discussion, I told him I would love to help him in the start-up as a fractional marketing executive, but I had no interest in being a founding executive, knowing what it took in hours, travel, and commitment. My kids were so young, and I knew I wasn't willing to dedicate the hours required in a start-up venture.

A funny dynamic happened after that meeting. He just kept calling me as if I was working for him. It was such an honor to know him and to receive calls from him that I just kept answering and engaging. In a tornado of activity over a couple of months and many conversations with business associates and my husband, I hesitantly accepted the SVP of Marketing role at an amazing start-up, reporting directly to the legend himself. It was the first time in my life I was hesitant. It wasn't a full-body-yes. It was different from normal nerves and anticipation that come with any new job. I wasn't sure how to be in two places at one time. The hesitation was around the uncertainty if I could do both well—be a great executive and a great mom. My consulting business gave me everything I needed at the time, high profile strategic projects, good compensation, and ability to be home based with the kids. Why was I leaving it behind? Was this a mistake or was this the right decision? I've learned that big life decisions take wise discernment, and you can only have as much discernment as you have wisdom at the time. Sometimes you just don't know until you jump in. You make the best decision you can make at that moment in time.

Note to Self

**In every season of life,
make the best decisions at that time.
Learn and build discernment muscles along the way.
Decisions are not always right or wrong.
They are simply decisions at the time.**

It was my first experience being a part of an executive team, reporting directly to the CEO and serving a board. It was exciting and terrifying all at once. The ability to learn the ropes from such a legend was like a master's degree in business, board management, and specifically software as a service (SaaS) technology investment models. He was brilliant in the way he managed the board, welcomed advice, listened intently to all opinions, and led with a passion and love for business and people. I was an observer, and I was coachable. I was a sponge soaking in everything around me. He took me under his wing and taught me this world. He taught me how to manage a board, think out of the box, and ask the right questions. He taught me how to be sensitive to egos, begin conversations, and negotiate. Most importantly he showed me how to do it all with integrity. He directed lawyers during negotiations to back down and stay with the intent of the deal. He was a master.

As amazing as this time was to grow and learn and work with some experienced leaders and investors, it was challenging too. I was naive and wanted to prove myself in this new ecosystem. I listened to every comment made by every board member and every executive. I took the comments as instant action items for myself, and I inflicted a ridiculously long task list on myself.

I am a producer. I'm excellent at creating and knocking out insane task lists. There is nothing more satisfying for me. I even take it a step further by getting as much done in the most efficient way possible. It's not only at work but with kids and even running errands on weekends. If there are fifteen things to get done, I'd line them up perfectly to get it all done in a minimum time frame. I would race back home looking for my trophy. I won. I got the most done in the most efficient way possible. Where is my trophy? Oh yeah, it was a race I created for myself and ran alone. Hysterical.

With that not necessarily sane mentality, in the first year of this leadership role, I created unachievable work and home task lists for myself. Then I achieved them all. I can laugh at it now, but at the time, it almost took me down physically. Literally, I was having chest pains, not sleeping, and hitting a wall. The stress and pressure I put on myself was not sustainable. It felt like everyone in my life had too high expectations or demands of me, but in reality, it was my own doing. I was the one putting too much pressure on myself, many in my life were just merely sharing ideas. They didn't necessarily mean for me to take full responsibility for them.

For example, if a coworker mentioned a marketing idea in passing, I added it to my list to either research or execute. If my family mentioned a need or an idea, it went on my list. At this time in my life, I had not learned to say no or delegate. The wall felt like a task list for ten, but it was all for me. The wall also felt insurmountable because so much of it was new. The working environment was new. The company and the job were new. And being a working mother was still relatively new.

There were two things I learned later that I would tell my younger self at this time. First, when you experience anything new, the first several months are the most stressful because there are so many firsts. Give yourself time and grace. Things get easier. Second, make sure everything on your list is truly necessary, and in the timeframe you set. Take a few items off. Push a few items out. Delegate a few. For me, it was my expectations of myself that were too high, not necessarily others' expectations.

**Hitting a wall doesn't always mean
you need to stop or bust through the wall.
Sometimes it means you need to lean on it
for a minute and catch your breath.**

In this new ecosystem of investors, advisors, and executive team members, I was the only woman on the executive team and board. I could not have been more welcomed or more supported. I was very aware that me being a woman could make others uncomfortable or act guarded. So, I spent a significant amount of energy making sure everyone else felt comfortable with me. A few of the male leaders also worked on their side to make me feel comfortable. Symbiotic energy is one of the challenges to achieving diversity.

**Diversity at the top takes effort.
It changes the dynamics in the room.
It is challenging for those who
have always been in the room
and for the new ones in the room.**

My femaleness was less of a disconnect than the greater home and child responsibilities that I had compared to my fellow executives. Most of the direct reports to the CEO had stay-at-home spouses or spouses with more work flexibility to take care of kids' schedules. I didn't. The way meetings were scheduled, and work travel was arranged was based on every executive having more freedom from home or kid responsibilities than I had. I planned the family and work logistics and schedules a week ahead. Last-minute decisions to jump on a plane for a business trip were easier for others but could rock my world in a million pieces.

When you are the minority, you usually adapt to the majority. I was in a man's world. If I wanted to play and be successful, I had to balance leaning into the masculine ways while still maintaining my authentic self and upholding my boundaries between work and home. Being present for my children daily was not something I was willing to sacrifice. I chose to work from home as much as possible, which wasn't as acceptable then as it is now. I was the only one that even wanted to work from home. Everyone else loved coming into the office. I think I was able to negotiate more flexibility because I overperformed. I made sure I was present for all the in-person meetings that were most important to my boss, our board, and my fellow executives, and the rest I did from home. I made sure I delivered everything and more under my area of responsibility and I supported my coworkers.

Note to Self

**Understand the rules of my environment.
I need to overperform and work harder
to gain respect and flexibility.
Don't underestimate the power of being kind
yet confident and working with others who
are also kind and confident.**

For the next decade, I worked with multiple companies within this investor's portfolio. It was high-growth, high-speed, and involved many mergers and acquisitions. It was exciting to work with so many different companies, entrepreneurs, and industries. The challenges of a $1 million company versus a $150 million company are very different. That first financial start-up built prepaid debit cards and was merged with another portfolio company that provided prepaid wireless refill cards in retail stores. Our top competitor acquired our company. As part of the acquisition, I agreed to stay as head of marketing for the new combined company for a few years. We became a global payment technology company transforming payment options for retailers, brands, and consumers. We created a new retail product category showcasing gift cards, wireless and debit cards in all the top retailers across the country from Walmart, Target, dollar stores, gas stations, grocery to drug stores. We were also working with some of the top financial companies, including American Express, Visa, and Mastercard. The marketing team was creative and innovative. Being a part of defining a new marketplace and working with so many great brands elevated my skill sets and broadened my perspective. There was never a dull moment.

As someone who loves to learn and grow, I soaked in as much wisdom as possible. I quickly learned the trickle-down effect of every decision and every move of the board, CEO, and executive team. I started realizing the power of each of our spheres of influence. One casual micro decision would take a company down a different trajectory. One bit of positive encouragement from a high-ranking executive changed a person's life. One negative assessment could crush a career. The smallest act of kindness or act of anger rippled into a hundred micro reactions. I watched the ramifications of an emotional executive yelling at a direct report and then that direct report lashing out at their direct reports. Negative impacts seemed to leak through an entire organization. It could happen in a positive way as well. I became acutely aware of how important choosing the right words and actions were to my coworkers, team, and family. Words are so important. When you have a horrible day at work you also tend to bring all the negativity home to your family. It was a ripple effect.

I realized the higher up you climb in the corporate world, the larger your sphere of influence becomes. There are more eyes watching you and being impacted by your decisions and your energy. I felt more accountable for my actions, words, and energy that I brought in a room, both at work and at home.

It became obvious that intentions matter, even when execution is not perfect. We all make mistakes in execution or fumble our words in conversations, but the intention usually shines through. In my role as a parent and an executive, what were my intentions? An ask of someone else can be driven by a need to control and feed your ego. It can also be with an intent to teach something and help another person grow. I watched leaders who had a desperate need to be "right", and some that were having open dialogue, taking accountability, and even apologizing when they made a bad decision. As I became more aware of my intentions, it changed the way I approached conversations with my team and my kids. The power of an apology when I was wrong created trust and gave my team and my kids permission to be wrong sometimes. It taught them to be accountable when they were wrong.

Note to Self

It's not always what I say but how I say it.
Words have tremendous power and ramifications.
Be intentional. Be aware and
accountable for my sphere of influence.
We all get it wrong sometimes. Apologize when necessary.

The professional and personal lessons were becoming more and more intertwined. The many years under my mentor reaffirmed for me how business lessons were also life lessons. He recognized and respected the human aspect of business. He confirmed what I believed. We all have a need to be heard, respected, trusted, and loved—both at work and at home. Although they are completely different environments, the human nature of both is similar. Understanding human psychology and relations is as important for success in business as the financials, legal structures, and strategies.

How we manage or don't manage our personal relationships, health, and finances in our personal life is usually a sign of how we lead and manage as business leaders. It is all interconnected. I had witnessed individuals dealing with major health issues and having to leave their jobs temporarily or even permanently. This was another sign for me to manage my stress and my health now before it was too late.

The venture investor that hired me became a mentor, friend, and someone I still go to today for advice and business opportunities. There is no way to capture everything I learned during those years. Here are a few of his pieces of wisdom that stand out as one substantial note to self:

- You don't have to be a jerk to be successful in business.

- Find a partner to do business together. It is lonely doing it by yourself. The CEO is a lonely job so make sure there is a right-hand person that they trust on their staff.

- Before you hire an executive for the first time, meet their spouse, preferably at their home. How they treat their spouse is how they will treat the employees after the honeymoon is over. How overstated or understated their home is says a lot about the person's priorities.

- Test ideas and products early before full production. Make sure "the dog is going to eat the dog food" before you invest millions. Interpretation: make sure consumers will buy what you are selling.

- Every business needs a value system and a board of trusted advisors. They will keep you from making dumb mistakes.

- Everyone needs to love and needs to be loved. Keep that in mind in how you treat people and communicate in both business and personal.

- Negotiations, especially when selling a company, can be intense. Find out the most important aspect of the deal to the other side and figure out a way to give it to them.

- Take negotiations offsite and get to know each other. Conference room discussions are completely different than breaking bread together.

- When investing in a founder's company, recognize this is the entrepreneur's baby. Again, find out the most important aspect of the deal for the entrepreneur and give it to them.

- When an entrepreneur brings you a business idea, be prepared that it may take twice as long and cost twice as much as they planned.

- You become who you hang out with. It is true in both personal and business. Surround yourself with the right people.

- Show as much respect for the front-line hourly employee as you do the CEO and board, because some of the best ideas that catapult the company forward will come from them. Ask questions and listen intently.

- You can't out crook a crook especially when you are not a crook. If you find you have fallen into business with a crook, get out as fast as you can.

- Don't do 50/50 deals, someone must be in charge.

- Two books everyone in business should read: *The Richest Man that Ever Lived* by Steven K. Scott and *The Sociopath Next Door* by Martha Stout, PH.D.

What I didn't know when it was first recommended to me was *The Sociopath Next Door* would be one of the greatest gifts to my leadership growth. The book states that one in twenty-five everyday Americans is a sociopath. They could be your colleague, boss, coach, teacher, politician, preacher, neighbor or even a family member. They can do literally anything at all and feel absolutely no guilt. They have no conscience. They cannot love. They usually do not hold long-term relationships. They use people and move on. They usually have a high degree of charisma that makes them more charming or interesting than other people around them. They may be more intense, more spontaneous, more complex, or even sexier than the average. They are smart enough to understand how to fake caring, empathy, and other emotions for a brief amount of time, but they truly are indifferent to the suffering of others. They live to lead, dominate, and win.

Learning this in my 30s was invaluable. Prior to this book, I thought sociopaths were serial killers only. I had no idea there was a level of sociopath that didn't kill but destroys people in their path. It is very common to find sociopaths in powerful positions, but they can also be in church, neighborhoods, or schools, and they are equally male and female. They may flatter you or give you a pitiful victim story to get you to do whatever they want you to do. Some will come across as pure bullies and create outrageous stories and lies to convince you to concur what their needs are at the time.

You can't change a sociopath. So don't waste time trying. You can identify them, try to avoid getting on their target list and manage around them, but you can't ever expect to have a good long-term working relationship with them. Once you understand what a sociopath is, then you will quickly look back in your life and identify she was one, he was one and oh, that is why they did what they did. It is fascinating and scary but better to know and be able to identify so you can exit stage left as quickly as an opportunity presents itself, or if it is a neighbor or family member you can just learn to put boundaries in place and lower your expectations of the relationship.

During this time in my career, I was also learning and growing as a parent. My kids were changing every day. They grounded me. I was amazed at how something I learned in business applied at home in parenting and vice versa. Raising two children with very different personalities and agonizing over what worked for one and not for the other gave me more understanding and empathy for different employee personalities that I was managing. My two very different worlds fostered skills for each other. Having kids and working was a positive not a negative. Everything I had been told or taught said being a working woman was sacrificing one for the other. I'm so glad I didn't listen.

Like a breath of fresh air, slowly but surely, there were more high-level working women with children and more men juggling dual income relationships thriving in the work environment. It was encouraging. I was no longer the only one at the top. Suddenly, I had one or two other women sitting at the executive table. It was refreshing and exciting. I also had several of my closest female friends that decided not to have kids and several who decided to stop working and stay home with their kids. I wish there was more support and less judgment for different choices. Like many, I experienced severe judgment, and the burden of assumptions from those who had made different choices. There were the deliberate gossip attacks, and then there were the innocent comments like, "My wife chose family over work," or "We didn't want someone else raising our kids, so she decided to stay home." There were moments of hurt and wonder, but luckily having my sisters, who had both chosen ambitious careers and are amazing mothers, as well as so many of my closest friends, minimized the negative feedback and reinforced my confidence in my choice to be a working parent. I was also empathetic for many of my stay-at-home friends who were feeling judged by working mothers. It seemed so ridiculous to me. It came back to how most humans have a difficult time respecting or accepting different opinions and different choices.

Note to Self

**You do you and be unapologetic
for your choices,
but let others do the same.**

TEAM DYNAMICS:
THE GOOD, THE BAD,
AND THE UGLY

Teamwork makes the dream work, and it also can kill the dream. I was quickly learning that a team is only as strong as its weakest link. If one individual is not holding up their area of responsibility, they negatively impact the whole team or they put more burden on other members. Even if one department within a company hits all its objectives or overachieves, if another department constantly misses their objectives, they bring down the entire organization. The company usually stumbles.

In one company, I was head of marketing, and the company had been working on a new release of our software product for several years. The CTO promised delivery dates repetitively every few months and missed every deadline, every time. The other departments including mine continued to deliver on their areas of responsibility, but success was limited due to one department's inability to deliver. The collective feeling of disappointment, anger, and frustration across the whole company was palpable. The pressure on every other department increased to try to make up for the one department's inability. I remember thinking to myself, there is no way the rest of us can overcompensate. There was no way a marketing spin could make up for not delivering to our customers over such a long period of time. I was right. It was a lesson for me in what can be fixed and what can't be fixed.

It's why I disagree with a common saying in corporate management, "Stay in your lane," meaning that the marketing department should focus on marketing and customer service should focus on customer service. Every department is interdependent. Therefore, creating a positive cross-functional team dynamic and hiring well across all departments is critical. It takes communication, respect, clear processes, and hand-offs so every department has specific deliverables and understands the co-dependencies. Most importantly, each department must be held accountable for delivering.

It applies to individuals as well. Different styles and personalities are great but carrying people that don't pull their weight is not acceptable. A sure way to lose your strong employees is to keep weak ones. There was one time I broke this rule in my career. I held onto a B player only because the company was in a hiring freeze, meaning if you lost an employee, you were not allowed to hire a replacement. In this situation, two hands were better than no hands. So, I kept my B player.

As a team leader, I learned to hire and manage around strengths and weaknesses to create more power to positively impact a company. I wanted every member of my team to have different skill sets to complement each other. I also hired to my weaknesses, not my strengths. For example, if my strength was speaking and presenting, I didn't need another person with the same quality. I needed someone who was superior in something I was weak in. To better the company, I needed to fill voids, not duplicate. I surrounded myself with people that think differently and even challenged my thinking. However, I quickly recognized that managing a team with great diversity in thinking, skill sets, and personalities made my job as a manager more challenging. As we all know, different personalities get on each other's nerves and can make collaborating a challenge. As the leader, helping them learn to interact and collaborate takes great effort. And in some cases, even teaching them how to speak to each other and understand each other can be beneficial. In the end, it is worth it. The team is stronger. The innovation is more creative. The impact for the company is greater.

Note to Self

Hire around my strengths and weaknesses.
Hire for diverse thinking.
My team will have a greater impact for the company.

———— ♀ ————

The team dynamics at the top were fascinating to me. Many executive teams and boards get it right and when they do, amazing progress is made. The vision is clear, collaboration is strong, goals are met, challenges are overcome, and execution is brilliant. When they get it wrong, the results can be detrimental.

Where I have witnessed it work well was when the board is a group of trusted advisors that have experience to guide a company to the next level, whatever that may be. Their experiences add value to the company. It may be the same industry experience. It may be similar product experience or relative partnering ecosystem. Or if the company is planning to go public, then they offer that wisdom. When board members have a vested interest in the success of the company and are a respected group, the executive team can bring their most complicated problems to them for advice, then the relationship is extremely valuable. In many cases, board members may disagree. I've been given opposing advice from two different board members. It is still great insight as there is never one way to solve a problem. It is up to the Chair of the Board and the CEO to take in all the advice and make the final decision.

Where I've seen it go wrong is when a CEO manages his executive team for quarterly board meetings and the purpose of the board meeting shifts to a presentation of how great the company is doing. This is a dangerous strategy. It serves no one when executives start spinning the story of their department more positively than reality. Inevitably, this results in misdirecting the board from its true purpose which is to help the executive team solve difficult problems and oversee objective completions for that particular season of the company. The CEO and executive team should be the ones running the company, not the board. When I have seen it reversed, it has never led to a positive outcome for the organization.

Boards, like other teams, need diverse thinking as well. When every board member has the same background, similar styles, same age bracket, same gender, there may be more agreements in the business discussions, but innovation, creativity and well thought out problem solving may be limited. Unfortunately, in my 30-year career, I personally have never served a board that had any diversity despite my best efforts to influence otherwise. I routinely suggested and even created a list of well qualified diverse board candidates. Each time, there was agreement and expressed gratitude. Unfortunately, there was never any action to make it happen.

CAN YOU HEAR ME NOW?

I had watched many different styles, relationships, and power in the decision-making room. I had been "taught" certain techniques as a female at the top to be heard—stand up, lower your voice slightly, make eye contact, lean in, pause, ask questions. There is the common joke that men have "selective hearing" in marriages, and everyone laughs. In the boardroom it is not funny.

Here's what happens: Jane vocalizes an idea or recommendation. It falls on deaf ears. Two hours later Dick vocalizes the same idea. Cheers, great idea, let's do it. Jane and Dick are at the same level. Many competent female executives and I have been Jane too many times. The first time it happens, you're disappointed, a little frustrated but hey, life isn't fair, and you're privileged to be at the table, so you move on. The important thing is the idea got approved. It shouldn't matter who got credit. So, you put your ego aside. The second time, you think you might be losing your mind. The third and fourth time, you muster the courage to point it out in a joking manner of course, as you don't want to hurt any egos. Then the fifth, sixth, seventh, eighth, and ninth time it happens, you get angry. It's exhausting and such a waste of energy.

Note to Self

Every role is important in an organization.
Show respect by listening to the originator of an idea.
Dynamics between the executive team
and board have significant impact.

—— ♀ ——

PAY INEQUALITY: WHO'S RESPONSIBLE?

After years in management, I had observed pay inequality more times than not. On teams that I inherited, the females were often paid less than the males in the same job with no justification. I found myself having to fight for pay equity and equality in almost every new position and company. It was exhausting and frustrating. I never set out to fight for pay inequality, but it was so rampant and felt so wrong, I felt I had to speak up. I was shocked because it was technically illegal, and I wondered how this could still be so widespread in corporate America. I won some battles and I lost many. I also started connecting the dots of how this phenomenon was happening.

Here is how a collision of factors changed my mindset around pay inequality and responsibility. I was interviewing candidates for a director position. I had two candidates scheduled back-to-back. The job salary range was $80,000 to $100,000. This was the guideline given to me by my human resources team, which reflected the average market value for the job. The first candidate was overly confident in the interview and when I asked how much he would need as a base salary, his answer was $110,000. I thought that was interesting given the published maximum for the job was $100,000. He had a solid resume, plenty of experience for the job, but not above average. So, why did he think he deserved above average pay, I wondered?

The next interviewee had a solid resume with slightly more experience than the previous person. She had a great personality but was a little sheepish. She was confident but nervous. The negative was she was overly thankful and overly apologetic. My last question was the same as I had asked the first candidate. Her answer was, "I really would love this job…and if possible…if not I understand…but if there was any way I could get $65,000…but if not, that is okay, I understand."

I cringed at the weak way she asked for less than she truly deserved. I was speechless. Her lack of confidence was irritating, not because I didn't have empathy and understanding of why she felt the way she did, but that I had hoped it was a thing of the past. She was more qualified than the first candidate. She wasn't even asking for the published minimum salary range for the job. I paused and thought for a moment. My job as the hiring executive was to represent the company's best interest and hire the best candidate in the most economical way. I chose to do something I had never done before in my career.

I said, "I'm going to step out for a moment and when I return, I am going to ask that last question again as if for the first time. In that time frame, I want you to reread the minimum and maximum salary for this job. I want you to reread your own resume and see that you are not only qualified, but you are close to being overqualified for this position. I want you to reassess your answer based on someone who deserves this job and is the best candidate for this job."

I left the room and gave her fifteen minutes to rethink.

I wanted to shake her by the shoulders and scream, "Ask for what you deserve. Be confident. It's okay. You will get it." I also wanted to shake him and say, "Get real with your experience and the market value of the job. You need to learn a little humility."

I walked back in the room, sat down, and asked the same question. She looked me in the eye. I gave her the silent nod saying you got this. She said, "I would need $85,000 minimum before I would accept this position." I said, "Are you sure?" She said, "Yes, I am sure." I hired her at $85,000. I could have gotten her at $65,000 and I would have paid her $100,000 based on her experience. Let that sink in for a moment.

I realized, in part, why salary inequity was continuing. Our society creates this dynamic of some feeling overly confident and some feeling under confident. There were so many messages I had received throughout my life saying you are lucky to be here, don't ask for more. It took years before I came to the realization that I deserve to be here just as much as anyone else and to be paid fair market value.

The way I see it now is when a female or male "shows up to the party" (i.e., an interview, meeting, relationship) feeling either inferior or superior, the problem begins. If a society tells one group more than another, they are not good enough as they are growing up, then their confidence is negatively impacted. It takes a lot of self-awareness and self-confidence to feel deserving of a promotion or a certain salary. Learning to have an unemotional realistic view of a job's market value and a rational assessment of your own resume with the confidence to ask for what is deserved is a skill set everyone needs.

As I started recognizing that market value for a job fluctuates as the supply and demand shift helped me take the emotion out of the equation. Companies' pay grades fluctuate for different positions. These aspects have nothing to do with my resume. They have to do with the job market as a whole and the demand within a particular industry.

My value to a company is based on my experience and contributions at any given time along with the marketplace dynamics at that time. We will know we have overcome the equality issue when we are able to talk about the job requirement, pay range in relation to the applicant's experience regardless of their sex, ethnicity, or physical appearance. Yes, it is already a law, but the law is not reality yet. We still have a long way to go.

I wholeheartedly believe we need both the masculine and feminine thought processes in decision-making positions and throughout entire organizations. The benefit of diversity is invaluable.

Note to Self

**Pay equality is both parties' responsibilities—
the company and the individual.
Micro shifts in both men and women are needed
to celebrate our differences,
recognize our unique superpowers,
and find equality in respect, value, and confidence.**

LEADERSHIP STYLES: FIND WHAT IS AUTHENTIC FOR YOU

I found much of corporate America encourages the "hustle culture at all costs" mentality. The hustle culture can get results. It is one way, not the only way. I have participated in the hustle culture many times. I have also seen where a pause before acting can be smarter in some cases. There are advantages in seeing the problem with more of a 360-degree view, creating new innovative solutions, and understanding how to inspire humans to do more with less or work smarter not necessarily harder. Both are valuable.

There are as many leadership styles as parenting styles. I have observed almost every kind. As much as I had hoped there was an obvious formula for leadership that I could mimic to guarantee powerful financial success for a company, I haven't found it yet. What I found is that there isn't one kind that drives great results. I have seen as many incompetent as competent leaders be rewarded financially. I've observed leaders who have punched a hole in a wall, cursed out employees, lied through their teeth, battled alcoholism, had affairs, and sexually harassed individuals yet received tremendous financial reward and even been praised in the business world. I've heard more times than I can count that "you must be an asshole to be a leader." I've seen ego-driven behavior and abuses of power drive horrendous short-term business decisions yet end up with what the business world would classify as a win. Incompetence at the top is not uncommon unfortunately, and something that millions have to deal with in their daily work environments. The good news is that kind, strong, competent leaders can also produce positive business results. They just happen to change lives and positively impact those around them at the same time.

In a world where we have choices, I looked for competent, conscious servant leaders to model my leadership style after. I chose those that successfully drove financial performance, delivered great products, and changed individuals' lives. Luckily there are many great examples of successful competent conscious capitalists to model after. I studied leaders like Robert Iger, Former CEO of Disney, Sir Richard Branson, Founder of Virgin, Indra Nooyi, Chairman and CEO of PepsiCo and Howard Schultz, Former CEO of Starbucks as well as leaders of great companies like Trader Joe's and Zappos. I gained so much respect for how they disrupted entire industries, created incredibly positive work cultures, took risks, and generated financial results and value for their companies. They were all different. I picked up something from each of them. They seemed to problem solve in a unique way and inspire those they managed. These leadership styles were ones that were worth modeling.

Note to Self

**Leadership with that powerful blend of
ingenuity, authenticity, confidence, and humility
inspires people to want to follow
and it also gets business results.**

As I was reading everything I could get my hands on about different leaders and companies, I discovered a shoe company called Toms® that was making the one-for-one business model famous. For every pair of shoes sold, they donated a pair to young children in developing nations. As a consumer, I fell in love with the company and their products. The shoes were comfortable and every time I bought a pair, I felt like I was doing good for a child on the other side of the globe. It was such a refreshing concept that business success could also be a force of good in the world. It was capitalism with purpose. It made so much sense to me. Doing good in the world and financial success could not only simultaneously exist but be a brilliant marketing story and drive company growth.

This led me to discover a book called *Conscious Capitalism* by John Mackey, CEO of Whole Foods Market and Raj Sisodia, Professor of Global Business. It was a new concept to me at the time. The basic theory of conscious capitalism is that organizations cannot only create value for the expected stakeholders like customers, employees, suppliers, investors, but can create value simultaneously for society and the environment. It adds two stakeholders to the equation that most companies ignore. To me, this speaks to the deep desire most of us have which is to be a part of something with a higher purpose than just making money.

One of the case studies in the book was about a carpet company, Interface, that was led by Ray Anderson, CEO, who transformed the company to adopt sustainable practices all the way through its supply chain. The sustainable effort became part of the vision and brand for the company. The carpet industry was notorious for non-sustainable practices. His competition thought he had lost his mind. He had critics from all sides. He proved everyone wrong. Interface became the first global flooring manufacturer to sell all products as carbon neutral across their full life cycle. Sustainability became part of their brand. The company experienced tremendous financial growth while concurrently adopting what appeared at first to be unattainable, sustainable practices in their operations. How could a carpet company be sustainable? One leader in one company made it happen. It was inspiring to me.

The book also had many examples of companies like Whole Foods, Google, REI, Patagonia, Costco, Panera, The Container Store and many more. Each story started with one or two leaders within the organization deciding to add an element of doing good to the business model. My first thought was I want to go work for a conscious capitalism company. Then I thought, what if I just make a difference where I am.

It occurred to me that any employee in any company has the potential to make a difference even if the company is not necessarily a conscious capitalist company. It can be something as simple as spearheading a health challenge, initiating a recycling program, or sponsoring a charity drive.

Note to Self

**Conscious capitalism is the epitome
of a win-win for all stakeholders.
I found my utopia, but I can make a difference
right where I am. We all can.**

MARKETING AND CULTURE: THE ART OF STORYTELLING, ASKING, AND LISTENING

As head of marketing, my job was quite literally to write the story of the company and its products for all the stakeholders—prospects, customers, employees, investors, and partners. I've always believed that great marketing must be authentic to the company culture and begins with asking the right questions and listening to the company's stakeholders.

Marketing is storytelling. In marketing and in life, words matter. A great brand story is respectful to the company's history, honors the customers it serves today, paints a clear picture of the future, and helps all stakeholders become ambassadors for the company. Finding the emotional connection that elicits engagement with buyers and pride from employees is what great marketers set out to accomplish.

Recognizing that no matter what business you are in, you are in the people business is an essential element in the process. Employees are people. Customers are people. Investors are people. *Humans are emotional beings.* They want to be a part of something with a higher purpose. Give them an emotional reason to buy. Give them an emotional reason to care about a team or a company. Great branding inspires people to buy products, attracts and retains employees, all of which have significant bottom line financial impact. Give them a reason to care.

In every company I had the privilege of serving, there was always something unique or special about the employees or the founder or the customers. It was like a treasure hunt for me to find the special emotional connection in each company that we could incorporate in the marketing. I called it the *soul signature* of the company. That relatable or inspiring golden nugget was what I was always looking for.

In one company, a restaurant software provider, we initiated a full rebranding project. When I arrived, the marketing message was focused on the technical aspect of their product only. It promoted the feature list of the software. Things like our software allows you to control inventory and food costs. The company was highlighting how it worked and what it did, which was all accurate, but there was so much more to the story. When I interviewed the employees and customers, I asked a ton of questions like what did it do for the customers and what were they most proud of about their company. I found this emotional connection to the history of the company, where they started, and who they served. There was this love and passion for the restaurant industry that was shared by all. Most of the employees had worked in restaurants. The company was a blend of foodies, restaurateurs, and software experts. We created a brand story around the entrepreneur nature of the company and highlighted all the amazing restaurants around the country that were their customers. The customers loved that we were highlighting their restaurants. As part of the marketing story, we also added the fact that 80% of our employees worked in restaurants before joining the software company. Our customers liked the fact our employees understood their business. They knew their pain points. It was relatable. It hit home.

When marketing honors employees and customers, it can increase marketing success exponentially. It can create a more positive work culture and increase customer retention. Employees and customers become an extension of your sales team, driving sales through referrals. If the company is doing good in the community or giving back in some way, then that becomes part of the brand story as well. It increases social media word of mouth. It can help with new employee recruitment. We weren't a conscious capitalism company, but we added a give back component to a high-profile national charity in our industry, No Kid Hungry. The employees sponsored a day of giving back to our local communities. We closed our offices for a day and employees volunteered to work for different charities. It served as a team building opportunity and gave employees a day out of the office. All of it combined, became a win-win for all parties.

Note to Self

**Storytelling and purpose inspire humans.
Doing good can increase marketing success,
employee, and customer retention.**

The art of storytelling isn't just part of marketing, it is part of leadership. How leaders communicate to employees, especially around future changes can raise morale or deflate morale. One of the most important things an executive team can get right is communicating a vision for all employees to rally behind. Employees can support a great vision, but without one they merely clock in and clock out or assume the worst. Every employee I have known wanted to understand the "why" behind what the company was trying to accomplish. One of the most difficult terrains to navigate in business and find the right words for is during mergers and acquisitions. I found myself in the middle of a merger or acquisition many times throughout my career.

When a company sells, or new investors come in, the lay of the land shifts. In general, employees and customers get uncomfortable and fearful as they don't know what it will mean for them. It is human nature, and many go to the worst-case scenario thinking:

I'm going to get fired, it's going to be horrible, they're going to raise the fees or discontinue a product. This negative scenario of self-talk turns into gossip and gains momentum quickly in a work environment. It can ruin a work culture overnight.

Great leaders can bring calmness and clarity in unsettling times by clearly articulating the facts and the benefits of a change. In one company, we did just that. We set and accomplished three goals each quarter and communicated regularly. Each employee knew what to expect and we started building trust one quarter at a time. In another company, we followed the same formula except the goals were never delivered by the product team and the direction of the company kept changing. The trust was broken between employees and leadership. The employees couldn't rely on what management was saying. The culture became very negative. What I learned was that words matter but doing what you say you are going to do matters even more.

Note to Self

**Employees want to understand the why of a change.
Help connect the past, present, and future
in a way they can understand and believe.
Words matter. Delivering on promises matters even more.**

Asking questions and listening weren't just a way of finding a more authentic marketing story and the heart of a culture, but they were also ways of improving processes and increasing efficiencies. Listening tours are a popular way many executives seek to understand, find key problems, and discover potential solutions. It is another great way to build trust. Learning to ask the right questions and listen for insights is an art I learned to appreciate along the way.

In every job, I always started with listening tours. Depending on the company, it could be visiting retail stores, warehouses, or simply meeting with different internal departments. Then I would meet with top customers, making sure it was a mix of satisfied and unsatisfied customers. I asked simple questions like:

- What is working and what is not working?
- Do you have any ideas for solving that issue?
- What do you love and what do you dislike?
- Why? Why not? What if...?

Let them talk and simply listen.

What would come next was always extraordinary. The customer comments would articulate key product improvements and insights into what the product promise needed to include. The internal employee meetings would bring light to culture issues, operational inefficiencies, and cross functional disconnects, but more importantly it uncovered solutions. Employees know what needs to be improved and, in many cases, how to solve them. I found listening and then empowering them to act always generated positive momentum.

In every instance, I would discover a slew of meetings, processes, paperwork, or rules that were useless or no longer necessary. When asked why are you doing this? The common answer I got was "we've just always done it that way." It may be a report that an employee is spending hours on every week creating that doesn't drive any wisdom or action. It could be a metric that is not serving the customer or the company. The immediate and biggest wins were simply stopping unnecessary work. Employees felt relieved, empowered and it opened their minds to ask questions going forward. For the business, we opened space for more impactful tasks and ideas.

One extreme example I came across was a report that an employee was spending two hours a week and eight hours once a month creating. To my surprise, no one was reading it or using it to better the company. I told him to stop. He was extremely uncomfortable not doing the report. This report had been produced for five years. He had taken it over from his predecessor. I said if someone needs it, they will let us know. No one ever asked for the report. They didn't even notice it had been stopped. We instantly saved him hours of work with no negative implications. Asking questions reveals opportunities to improve the business.

I stole this business discovery and adopted it as a parent. I asked the same type of questions of myself. Many times, my answer was because of the status quo, or because every other parent was doing it. There were several things I signed my kids up to participate in because other parents told me I "should." Luckily, my kids had the courage to challenge me on a few things that just didn't fit their personality. As soon as they brought it to my attention, I knew they were right, and I was wrong. We slowly weeded out those activities and just started saying no to things we didn't want to do. It was life changing.

Note to Self

Ask the right questions in business and in life.
The answers may surprise you.
Say no to things that are not serving a greater purpose.

HAVING DIFFICULT
CONVERSATIONS

Finding the right words and tone to have difficult conversations can have a surprising positive impact for individuals as well as company culture. It is one of the most difficult skills to develop, but when you get it right, it can quickly become a differentiator as a leader, since so many people avoid these conversations at all costs. Many leaders use silence, sarcasm, or passive aggressive behavior in lieu of a difficult conversation – all of which do nothing to help an employee improve and can quickly degrade the work culture.

The dread and anticipation of difficult conversations is usually worse than the actual conversation. First, I learned to look at the facts of the situation while also emotionally detaching. It wasn't about me. It wasn't about my performance. It was my job responsibility as their manager to give them constructive feedback that helped them grow. In business, a job has certain responsibilities and requirements. At the most basic level, your job is to fulfill those minimum responsibilities and of course great employees fulfill those and so much more. You must do the job you were hired to do. Period. At the end of the day, if an employee is not performing their job duties, you owe it to the employee to tell them.

In terms of the tonality of the conversation, I always start with what they were doing well. Then in as few words as possible, I would tell them what they needed to work on and why it was an issue. I tried to always give specific and recent examples. When appropriate I would coach them on how they could have done it differently.

In most cases, the employees were completely unaware or in denial of their weakness. Many had never been given constructive feedback. Their self-perspective was different from reality. It can be as simple as bringing it to their attention. Most conversations resulted in positive turnarounds. In other cases, it took far greater effort and time or a termination of employment. In every case the conversations resulted in a better employee and/or a better work environment.

The flip side is true as well. Learning to accept candid feedback from bosses and my team members broadened my self-awareness, but more importantly helped me become a better manager. Defensiveness is often the first reaction to feedback, but once you start understanding the benefits, you start welcoming it. Part of most executive programs is the requirement for personality and leadership assessments as well as 360-degree feedback appraisals. You get used to being told what you can do better. Believe it or not, I arrived in a season where I not only craved the feedback but appreciated it.

One boss told me that when someone else asks or suggests anything about marketing, I respond defensively. He was exactly right. I adjusted. One of my team members told me once that she thought I might be intimidating to another employee from another department. At first, I thought she was joking as I thought I was overly kind and welcoming. I asked for more details and when she gave me more, I was able to see it. I adjusted immediately as that was not my intent. Be open to constructive feedback and criticism.

Note to Self

**Learn how to give and receive constructive feedback.
It is worth the initial discomfort.
It helps all parties and improves culture.**

———— 💡 ————

TIPS AND TRICKS
FOR MANAGING PEOPLE
AND STAYING SANE

Mentoring the next generation of leaders is one of my absolute favorite things in the work environment. One of the first pieces of advice I offer is to *add value*. I've always found the quickest way to get promoted is to become more valuable to my boss, my teammates, and the company. I would listen, observe, research, and act on things I saw that need to be improved. I tried to offer solutions to problems. Things like volunteering to lead a cross-functional team to solve a problem the company has been struggling with for many years. Taking a task off my boss's list. Finding ways to make doing business with the company easier for our customers. I even tried to make the job easier for my predecessor.

As a boss, I loved employees that were proactive versus reactive. The ones that brought ideas to you for improvements while others would only do what you asked and nothing more. The employees that would lead before they were even in a leadership position were always the ones that got my attention. Every level and every position has an opportunity to improve processes, cultures, and even the bottom line. Look for ways to add value and help others.

The reverse is true as well. Ask for help when you are struggling with a problem. You don't have to figure it all out alone. Reach out and ask your boss or a coworker to help you brainstorm a solution. So many employees suffer in silence. They think they must do it all themselves. Asking for help is not a sign of weakness, it is a sign of wisdom. Communication and collaboration can be the quickest way to get a project done. It can also help the overall culture of the company.

As companies and cultures shift, it may impact your job within the greater company. Learning to depersonalize it by seeing the bigger picture can help tremendously. A company is a matrix and an independent entity that should be in constant process of reevaluation and change to ensure it is running in the most efficient way and growing at a pace that is right for that season. If I am not making a difference for a company, then I have no business being there. If a job is destroying my personal life, then I must leave. If I am not giving and receiving simultaneously, then fulfillment stops, and it is time to move on. If a job is no longer needed for the company, then the company may need to eliminate the position. It's not personal. It's simply change.

Note to Self

Add value by solving problems that need solving.
Be a leader before you are a leader.
Your needs and the company's needs will shift.

One of my favorite tips I share with my team members is the 'badass' rule. Every month or so, I would ask myself if someone new, a badass, came in tomorrow and took my position, what would she or he do better? This made me look at everything with a fresh perspective, while igniting my competitive nature. It also challenged me as a leader. The longer you stay in one position, the more likely you get complacent which is dangerous. It kept me from losing my edge.

Also rethink how you see competition in business. Many to a fault focus on a direct competitor in the marketplace, obsessing to the point of almost derailing the company in attempts to match a competitor offering or style. Knowing your competition is important in business but focusing on your customers, overall market trends, and constantly improving your product, is far more important. The real competition could be entrepreneurs that are not even in the market yet. They have no baggage. They don't have to worry about an existing customer base or upgrading old technology. They can look at the problem with a fresh perspective. They are the ones that could disrupt the marketplace and blindside established businesses in mature markets.

To get my teams into this type of entrepreneur mindset, I would take them through the "white piece of paper" exercise. Imagine you have nothing to lose and that any of your perceived limitations, like budget or time, are not there. What would you do for the business? Pretend you are the two entrepreneurs in a garage designing something that will make our product obsolete. What would you build? What marketing tactic would you execute?

This exercise frees the brain to be truly creative and innovative. It also takes the victim mentality out of the equation. Many employees like to blame budgets or bosses as the reason why they can't do something. When you go through this exercise there is no one to blame. The outcomes of this exercise are different every time. Sometimes an innovative solution arises that the team would have never pondered and sometimes the team gets back to the original budget and plan but with greater confidence and accountability.

Note to Self

Practice the badass rule as often as necessary.
Brainstorm solutions as if you had a clean slate.

HAVING A CONVERSATION
WITHOUT HAVING
A CONVERSATION

For the extreme high anxiety times, sometimes visualization exercises, spiritual conversations, and prayer meditation work the best. These techniques helped me deal with negative situations without becoming bitter, angry, or playing victim, as that was not my authentic nature.

First is a meditation visualization that I added to my existing 20-minute morning practice. Every morning before I start work, I visualize a bright light streaming from above through the crown of my head and down through my entire body while my feet are planted solidly into the ground. Then I visualize all that positive white light going out of me to others I interact with throughout the day. Then, the most important part, I visualize a protective boundary around myself that takes any negative energy coming at me and bounces it back to the person sending it. It sounds crazy but it helped me survive some extremely negative situations and negative people. It's like a visualization of the classic principle of karma. If a truly negative, ill-intentioned person is sending out negative energy, it bounces back to them. People who are sending positive energy get positive energy back to them. You get what you put out in the world.

The reason this visualization helped me so much is because I never wanted to become like them and be ruthless or negative in retaliation. One of the hardest things in life is to resist fighting and lashing back at negative people. I also didn't want to wish ill will on them necessarily. I did want them to be accountable for their actions. It doesn't always happen right away, but I do feel we all get a little bit of karma served back to us eventually. I've seen it take years and I've seen it happen in an instant. The timing is neither for us to control nor to judge.

The second technique I use all the time is to have conversations with individuals' higher selves versus in person. This proved to be very effective for me. This technique was especially effective in a hierarchy situation, when you have issues with someone that is higher than you in a hierarchy organization. Even though we all want to believe we can stand up to unethical behavior and speak the truth, unfortunately there are still many work environments where we can't. I could say authentically in a "spiritual" conversation what I felt. It helped me vent honestly and not have to worry about being so careful with my words. It also did not have ill intent toward them, but asked for self-awareness and accountability for their actions. The conversation would go something like this, "You know what you are doing is wrong. Your higher self knows you are lying. This isn't going to serve you or the people around you well. Do what is best for your highest self and the highest self of those around you. You have the power to do better so do better." Then I surrender the issue to powers far greater than I and the individual's choice of free will.

The last technique I use often, especially with my kids. Instead of intervening in their journey, I send them light and love to their highest self and empower them to make their own choices. Visualize a protective barrier around them for safety and ask their spiritual guides to be with them and then surrender the situation. Don't try to control it. Let them experience rough times, failures, or even bad decisions. We all have our own personal life journey. From skinned knees to facing fears, all teach us more about ourselves. The confidence gained from difficult experiences, the mighty muscles of "I can do it" grow and on the other side they are stronger and a little wiser.

Discernment wisdom is a gift of an experienced life, knowing when to vocalize your opinion and when to keep quiet and let things play out. For me, most of it has come from my intuition, my knowing. Daily meditation and prayer, the quiet time of stillness and connection to the Divine, helps me stay centered. When I sit quietly by myself, decisions become clearer.

Note to Self

**Sometimes a spiritual conversation
or a visualization exercise
is the better choice over an in-person conversation.**

———— ♀ ————

This too shall pass has been a mantra I have found invaluable during both the good and the difficult times, pausing just enough to feel it all and to process it all. We need to acknowledge, be present, enjoy and celebrate the good times. Reflect and remember how you did it and what you thought before, during, and after the accomplishment as this too shall pass.

Unfortunately, we must sit in the heartbreak, grief, betrayal, and loss as it is part of every life. I've learned to let it move through me to get on the other side. Every person and every scenario has a different time frame. The challenge is to not let it consume you for a long time, never push it down or internalize it. For some experiences, it even takes short term numbing to get through it as it can be too painful to consume without support. Just don't numb it forever. Ask for whatever help you need. Deal with it and don't stay in it any longer than necessary as the world needs your light back.

As I got older, worked in many different companies, and watched my kids experience the world, my perspective of good and bad times shifted. When I was battling a difficult leadership challenge with other great leaders, I found it was truly rewarding. Staying late in the office and white boarding a thousand scenarios and collaborating with extremely talented leaders was thrilling. I learned to love the challenge of difficult conversations with employees that needed improvement or growth. The lack of sleep and pressure of putting on a million-dollar event with the right team was fun and exciting. Perspective is everything and as you grow, your perspective shifts.

Note to Self

**This too shall pass.
Be present for both the good times
and the bad times,
even shift your definition.**

Lastly, here are a few philosophies I've adopted along the way that are simple, yet the most difficult to practice every day. Keeping these top of mind makes work life so much more rewarding and more effective.

- Agreements with yourself and with those around you from my favorite short book, *The Four Agreements*, by Don Miguel Ruiz.
  - Be impeccable with your word.
  - Don't take anything personally.
  - Don't make assumptions.
  - Always do your best. Your best looks very different each day.
- Don't be an "askhole." No one respects askholes. There are two types.

- A person that only calls for an "ask" but never gives in a relationship.
- One who asks questions in a group setting with the intent to humiliate another.
- Always praise in public and discipline in private.

• Leave a job on good terms.
- The majority of career opportunities come from those you have worked with before.
- Give a job your best until the last day. The respect you gain is worth it.
- Even in a lay off situation, taking the high road will be remembered.

• Remember you always have choices even when it feels like your back is against the wall.
- You can stay or you can go.
- You can choose to take the high road, even when others don't.
- You can make micro shifts to make a situation better.
- We teach others how to treat us by what we allow, what we stop, and what we reinforce.
- When you accommodate unrealistic requests, you are telling others they can continue with their unrealistic requests.
- If you volunteer for extra work or covering for a coworker, you will always be the one overburdened on the team.

• Corporate layoffs hit individuals emotionally and financially.
- Give yourself and others tremendous grace through the process.
- Reach out to others for support and opportunities.

• Give to others without any expectation of return, otherwise, it isn't really giving.
- Giving isn't meant to be an equal exchange.
- Drop the scorecard.

- Gossip for good versus gossip for ill intent.
  - Spread a best-case scenario during a merger and acquisition when others are assuming the worst.
  - Talk about something good a coworker did.
- Laughter is a management technique, stress reducer, and creativity booster. Work doesn't have to suck.
  - Learn to laugh at yourself and don't take things too seriously.
  - Find your people in every company. The ones that make you laugh.

The more I practice these philosophies the more I enjoy my career and my life. Even with the best practices, change is always around the corner.

RETHINKING THE HUSTLE:

A GLOBAL PANDEMIC, SOULBBATICAL,
AND GETTING COMFORTABLE
WITH THE UNCOMFORTABLE

CHANGES EVERYWHERE AND THE SHIFT HEARD AROUND THE WORLD

Change has been the only constant in my life. My kids' needs and desires change as they age. My perspective shifts as I grow and experience more in life. Most of my career has been in the venture capitalist or private equity funded technology industry which by nature creates massive changes with significant investment, high growth, mergers, and acquisitions. Bosses, coworkers, and company names change frequently. It can be stressful and overwhelming if you fight it, or it can be exciting and exhilarating if you accept it. I have found the more I accept and even expect change, the more my stress level reduces.

In my early 50s, I have a much calmer reaction to the ups and downs in business and in life. I don't react to the chaos or emergencies of others. I have also worked with almost every type of personality, the great ones, the good ones, and the not-so-good ones. There truly isn't much that surprises me or stresses me out professionally. It is a good feeling.

I was a willing participant in the hustle culture for over thirty years. I set audacious goals, produced at an epic pace, and was on an airplane every other week. Like many, I ran on adrenaline and never thought twice. Now, I work smarter, not necessarily harder. I focus more on "continuous improvement." In the work environment, there is never an end date to seeking improvements and there is always room for another level of betterment. Focusing teams on weekly and monthly improvements around productivity, efficiency, and collaboration has consistently had more impact on bottom line results for the company and driven the right mindset for every individual to be constantly seeking a better way of doing things. Making the micro shifts seems to be more sustainable and less emotionally draining for my teams. The small wins give us a little dopamine and encourages repeat behavior. I have found micro goals create macro impact for the individuals and the greater company.

Note to Self

Change is the only constant in life.
I can fight it or accept it.
Micro goals and micro shifts seem to be
more sustainable and have macro impacts.

The business world was changing dramatically. There were so many great new leaders emerging that gave a whole new perspective of smarter more authentic leadership, healthier marriages, and better work and life integration that included rest and fun as part of the formula: Sara Blakely (Founder of Spanx), Jesse Itzler (Author, co-founder of Marquis Jet, co-owner of Atlanta Hawks), Amy Griffin and Anna Doherty (Partners of g9 Ventures), Kat Cole (Investor, President COO of Athletic Greens), Daley Ervin (Ultra athlete and Managing Director of Engage), Jessica and Garrett Gee (The Bucket List Family), Arianna Huffington (CEO of Thrive Global) and so many more. Respect for female led businesses was growing. Female politicians were running countries extremely well. Female entrepreneurs were creating multi-million and some billion-dollar businesses. Many companies were doing great things to create better work cultures and learning the traditional work model wasn't the only option. There were new venture capitalist firms focused on investing in minority-led businesses. There was some positive movement in diversity at the top, not enough, but positive.

For a brief few months, there were three other women sitting with me in board meetings, making the executive team 40% female. For the first time in my career, my boss's spouse was an executive. They had two young kids and had to juggle responsibilities equally as they both had high-level jobs and traveled. It was so refreshing to witness. Finally, it felt like progress, and I had several co-executives with lives like mine. We were all juggling similar balls. Our head of sales was one of my favorite people in the world that I had ever worked beside. He led with so much self-awareness, integrity, humor, and intelligence. Our sales and marketing relationship was a true partnership in opposition of the normal tension filled relationship many organizations promote between sales and marketing.

It felt like there was a massive awakening and shift for a better definition of leadership that was inclusive and respectful of both masculine and feminine traits, not just in my small area of the world but in the larger global world. In the beginning of my career, all leadership books were written from a male perspective, and now there are business leadership books that are written from a female perspective. The tolerance for the "patriarchy only" way was waning.

There was a call for women to lead like women instead of adopting leadership traits that were not authentic to them. Even more importantly, there was a call for male leaders to learn some traits from successful female leaders. The language of leadership was shifting to include traits like intuition, empathy, resilience, purpose, and understanding. There was bottom-line evidence these leadership traits were effective.

Minorities were changing the game and demanding respect instead of receiving oppression. Many brave people were speaking up for the first time. There was also a very aggressive, desperate clinging to control by the old regime that was playing out by those in power positions feeling the shift.

The biggest shift, the COVID-19 global pandemic, instantly changed our work and home lives with forced unwanted restrictions on all of us. It was the first truly global shared experience in my lifetime. The whole world was slowing down. The polarity of politics in America was at an all-time high. It was astonishing to watch it all unfold. The fighting, the bullying, and the horrific hate. I felt myself shifting my very extroverted life to more of an introverted life. I didn't share the same beliefs as all those that were fighting each other. I didn't agree with either party and thought the news was a disservice to us all. I stopped watching the news for several years. I focused my attention internally to my family, my health, and my life. My kids were suddenly back home unexpectedly, and we were all trying to digest what was happening and how long this restricted world was really going to last.

Professionally at the time, I was working as Chief Marketing Officer, CMO, of a restaurant management software company owned by a private equity fund. We had been battling through the pandemic which had hit our restaurant customers hard. We had to lay off many amazing employees. It was emotional and sad. I had gone from being on an airplane every other week with team members in five different cities to laying off most of my team and not traveling at all. I felt I was handling all the normal stress very well. I was used to juggling multiple things in my life but the transition to empty nester was hitting me harder than expected. I loved my career, but I was bored. I wasn't learning anything new. Managing through COVID felt like every day was Groundhog Day. It felt like running hard in a circle going nowhere. I am addicted to growth, progress, and improved efficiency. The COVID period felt stagnant, repetitive, and unproductive. I was very proud of how our leadership team was choosing to lead our company through the pandemic, it just wasn't rewarding. Life was suddenly quieter.

It felt like everything was shifting and no one knew what was going to happen next. We were all asking questions. What was propaganda and what was real? How long was this going to last?

I turned my focus inward as that was all it felt like I could control. I decided to invest in a life coach for the first time in my life. I thought a third-party perspective could be very helpful. Our relationship started as a reader-author one. Years ago, I started a habit of reaching out to an author if their book had made an impact on me. I know how difficult it is to create as an artist or write a book as an author. It's a very creative and introverted experience and then you suddenly put your creation out to be judged by all, one can feel very vulnerable. Authors are artists and they need positive feedback like every human. When you love a book, tell the author! When you love art, dance, or music, tell the artist! I read a book, *Soulbbatical*, by Shelley Paxton and I related to her story of leaving corporate America and starting her Soulbbatical movement. I sent her an email and thanked her for writing the book. We began to have a few conversations and a few months later I hired her as my coach.

Note to Self

**The whole world got quiet and then I got quiet.
Time to tweak a few things.**

———— ♀ ————

And so, the "Soulbbatical" while working full-time began.

A DEEPER AWARENESS:
MAKING A FEW MICRO SHIFTS

What is a Soulbbatical?

According to Shelley Paxton, author of *Soulbbatical* and my coach,

"It is a way of being and movement. It's about living and leading from a place of authenticity and courage. It's about realizing that a fulfilling life means creating what you really want versus settling for what you think you should. It's leaning into your purpose to unleash your wildest potential and impact in the world. It's about becoming Chief Soul Officer of your own life, taking responsibility for nurturing both yourself and your soul."

It aligns with so many things I had preached over the years but wasn't necessarily doing fully for myself. It didn't mean quit your job and move to a farm, although those were thoughts I did entertain for moments. For me, it was about exploring outside of the roles that had defined me for so many years—mom, CMO, aunt, and problem-solver. It was about pausing and asking myself what truly gives me joy and what no longer serves me in this next season of my life.

Having a coach brought me a fresh third-party perspective to see what I couldn't see for myself. During our first session together, Shelley made some observations—I needed more self-care, joyful experiences, celebrations, and less problem-solving.

I'm an overachiever, so I'm harder on myself than any other person could ever be. I wasn't good at giving myself permission to take a break or rest. I tended to run on adrenaline and was in a heightened state of fight or flight mode given the roles I had chosen to play at work and at home. I also tend to be extremely loyal and empathetic to others' situations, which can be good for others but not so good for me. The highest-level description from my Enneagram personality assessment revealed that I think like a 6 - prepare for the worst, feel like a 4 - need to feel authentic and unique, and act like an 8 - need to be in control and avoid weakness. Sounds right.

The Enneagram is a system of personality typing that describes patterns in how people interpret the world and manage their emotions. It features a nine-pointed diagram to illustrate how the types relate to one another. Assessments like Enneagram and others are used in the corporate world to understand candidates, team dynamics, and provide greater self-awareness for individuals. They can provide insight into why we do what we do.

Shelley and I focused first on my addiction to playing the role of problem solver in my sphere of influence. Bring me your problem and I will help you solve it. Problem-solving was like a drug to me. I was good at it, which just encouraged it more. However, being the problem-solver, and in that rescuer role in both my professional and personal life was taking a toll on me. Secondly, she brought to my attention that I did not celebrate my accomplishments. I loved celebrating other people's accomplishments, but never paused to celebrate my own. I simply marked off goals as I accomplished them and then set new ones. My husband was even worse at celebrating. What a team! We both worked, accomplished, and worked some more. For me, it was my way of staying humble. By not acknowledging my accomplishments, I could never become arrogant. I despised arrogance. But I was too far along on the non-celebration spectrum. It wasn't healthy. I truly never realized it until that moment at age 51.

In an instant, a memory came back to me as a child. It was report card day in grade school. I had made straight A's and I felt relieved and proud. After school, I ran to the car with glee to show my mom. She quickly said, "Great job honey, but let's not say anything as others may not have gotten straight A's and we don't want them to feel bad." Made sense to me. I certainly didn't want to make anyone else feel bad. One little comment set up a lifetime of downplaying. It triggered an overcompensation on my part. I downplayed all my accomplishments or promotions. I kept them to myself or would have a small little celebration in the privacy of my home. Now that it was brought to my attention, I could shift. Sometimes that is all it takes: awareness.

Then we discussed the imbalance I lived with of giving and not allowing myself to receive help. Years of prioritizing my kids schedules and needs over my own and prioritizing my boss's, employees', and company's needs over my own needed to shift. I was so comfortable with giving but was so uncomfortable with receiving. I know this is something many can relate. It was aligned with that belief system I had adopted somewhere along the way of not wanting to owe anyone anything. If you had me over for dinner, then I would have you over for dinner at least two times. If you needed to borrow $100 from me and owe me that was fine, but I could never ever borrow money from someone else. Where do we pick these beliefs up that we carry with us for a lifetime? If we let go of the old beliefs that are not serving us well, we open ourselves up to more enjoyment in our everyday lives.

My coach and I also discussed the idea of taking some time off from corporate America. I couldn't even consider the idea at first. It seemed insane to me. Being a CMO was a significant part of my identity. It wasn't my only role in life, but it was a significant role. I couldn't fathom what I would do without the demands of an executive job or the idea of negative cash flow personally. Also, I had a deep love and passion for my marketing career. Why would I walk away from a great career? I loved working. My career has given me so many amazing experiences, from travel to professional events to great friendships. It was too much for me to even consider. So, we tabled the idea of leaving my job and continued with the micro shifts.

The problem solver stopped problem-solving for everyone. I learned to change the conversations in many of my relationships. Instead of problem-solving, I would ask something as simple as, "What do you think you should do?" or "What are you doing to change the situation?" I worked on training myself to pause and not say anything. I took a break from some relationships and in others I simply shifted the conversations. I just listened and let them think through it and figure it out for themselves, which in the end was more valuable for them. They gained confidence. I realized so much about myself and others through this simple micro shift. I let go of my need to be a problem solver and the burden I had put on myself. By the way, it had nothing to do with the people in my life. It was all me. I still love to problem-solve. I just stopped problem-solving for the repeat offenders—the ones that call with the same problem no matter the date. They literally tell the same victim story, and they never apply your solution to their life because they are stuck in victim or martyr mode. So, it becomes exhausting for you and completely unproductive for them. Those are the ones I gave up. The relationships where there was progress and mutual give and take, I kept. Those are the rewarding ones.

Then there was learning to celebrate. Comical really when I think about it. I started by going backwards. I had completed every bucket list I had ever created in my life, and I rarely celebrated. One of my best friends and soulmates really helped me in this department. She celebrated with me. I also had many solo celebration moments. Cheers to me, I did it. I climbed the corporate ladder, raised two amazing humans, survived a few sociopaths, married to a great guy for 25-plus years, mentored many and I am a relatively healthy active 50-something year old. Yay me. It was empowering to just say it out loud to myself, "I did it." Celebrating our small wins and our big wins is such an important habit to adopt.

Note to Self

**Giving myself permission to receive.
Letting go of the need to be the problem solver
gives others the skillset to problem-solve for themselves.
Celebrate along the way.**

———— 💡 ————

I also started doing a lot more self-care: more sleep, massages, movie-watching, and spending as much time outdoors as possible. I even began asking myself, what extracurricular activities do I want to do as if I was one of my kids? Guitar lessons, soccer, tennis, pickleball? Then it hit me, horseback riding lessons. I had always been drawn to horses and admired them for as long as I could remember but I had never taken the time for lessons. There were reasons—the expense and the time. In the ballet years we literally were not allowed to do anything else physically that would negatively impact our "trained" muscles. Ballet trains muscles to turn out. Equestrian activities train muscles to turn in. I also wanted to learn how to care for a horse as I had this fantasy of owning a horse one day but wasn't sure if I wanted the emotional risk or expense. I get extremely attached to animals and when I lose them, it's just hard.

Through a referral, I found a trainer. She had one lesson time that was going to open next month. It was 9 a.m. on Wednesday morning. Right in the middle of my work week. Impossible I thought, and then without hesitation I said yes. Then she said, "By the way I'm not sure what kind of lessons you were looking for, but I teach barrel racing." Pause. She explained to me that if you can do barrel racing then you will learn complete control of a horse. I said yes. What in the world? *From ballet to boardroom to barrel racing.* Why not?

I assumed I would have to cancel half the lessons due to my work demands but was going to give it go. I blocked my work calendar on Wednesday morning for the next several months. I showed up at the barn at sunrise and helped with the daily feeding, watering, and cleaning of twenty horses and then at 9 a.m. I groomed and tacked the riding lesson horse and took my lesson. I was CMO of a multi-million-dollar technology company and I was voluntarily shoveling horse poop out of horse stalls every Wednesday morning. I loved it. It grounded me. I watched the sunrise over the farm, and I learned the unique personalities of twenty horses every week. I slowly learned how to barrel race, but I learned so much more.

The horses reaffirmed my belief in the power of energy and intuition. They are powerful 1000-pound animals that are incredibly aware and sensitive. They can feel a fly land on their hind quarters. They can hear a human heartbeat from four feet away. In the wild, horses will synchronize their heartbeats to the other horses in the herd to sense danger more quickly. Horses feel human energy which is why they are so brilliant as therapy guides. Somehow, they know what you are thinking. If I arrived at the barn, stressed, and worried, it never went well. The horse would resist everything I did. When I arrived with "good", calm energy, it was always a great ride.

In one lesson, I was cantering the horse in a tight circle and became frustrated as the horse kept dropping back into a trot. Technically, I was doing everything correctly, meaning my hands, reigns, legs and calling for the horse to canter. My trainer said, "You're not thinking right. You are not committed to the canter in your mind." I thought, how the hell does the horse know what I am thinking? The horse knows. Sure enough, we did the same exercise again and I changed my mind, my thoughts. Perfect. I recalled a self-help book stating, "Change your thoughts, change your life." It took a horse to show me how true that saying really is.

Over the first six months I only had to cancel one lesson due to work meetings. For years, I had worked an insane number of hours every week and played catch up on weekends. It had never occurred to me that I could take a break in the middle of the work week for something that gave me joy. Interestingly, I was more productive on that day. Oh, how we limit ourselves with our belief systems.

Note to Self

More self-care makes me more productive.
Fit the joyful dreams into the schedule.
If we trust energy and intuition as much as animals do,
humans would be much more evolved.

MORE TIME HOME:
PURE HEAVEN

During the pandemic, like everyone, I had more time at home, which was lovely. I got back to my morning meditation on my screened-in porch before the barrage of Zoom calls began. It's my Zen spot with a view of nature. I love the great outdoors, trees, firepits, animals, and mountains.

My favorite place is my mother-in-law's mountain house in northeast Georgia. It is a little piece of heaven and our family getaway. It is where we exhale and get to be in nature with no neighbors in sight. There is something incredibly special about the mountain house and the land. It is spiritual for me. It is where I feel spiritually connected, in the middle of nature's magical ecosystem. As soon as we hit the driveway, my senses light up and the stress rolls off my back. Over the last thirty years, it has been our escape from the hustle and bustle of work, school, and sports. It has been where we have connected to each other at a deeper level. We pause and watch the sunsets, play card games, and breathe in the fresh mountain air. It's family and friend time. I often think about how my mother-in-law built this home for her family over forty years ago, not knowing how much joy it would bring so many extended family members, friends, and acquaintances. My father-in-law, in his hysterical eccentric way, decided to build a six-story tower next to the house in a friendly competition with his wife. He elicited my husband's help to design it. They built it with their own hands and with a few friends. It's special. Forty years later, it is our kids and extended family's favorite quirky element on the property. I like to call it the unexpected generational joy effect.

Note to Self

**Sometimes when you build something for one
it becomes a gift for many.
Nature is my spiritual place.**

My love for the mountains in general has grown over the years. It represents cooler weather, a reprieve from the norm, and epic views. My favorite vacations shifted to Montana, Utah, and Colorado versus the beach. Hiking in the Blue Ridge Mountains and chasing local waterfalls with girlfriends became more frequent. The quaint small town and the gorgeous lake community nearby have been calling my name more and more often. As empty nesters we spend more time up there now. It represented safety during the pandemic, away from the crowds. Maybe there is a little more to my ever-increasing love of the mountains. Maybe it is the obvious analogy of climbing the corporate ladder. It was a mountain of unexpected trails, trials, and false summits. I didn't realize how difficult it would be and the view at the top wasn't what I expected. When I got there, I felt a sense of accomplishment but also a sense of responsibility to 'clean up' the trail for others who may follow a similar path.

As one option for my next season, I started dreaming of leadership team-building workshops and women's weekend retreats in the mountains to inspire people to get back to nature, pause and rethink, refresh, and rejuvenate their relationship with themselves, their families, and their teams. Maybe even rethink their careers. I've always thought more business should be done outside. Get out of the office. Nature inspires.

Nature elements like waterfalls, mountains, lakes, forests, and beaches produced a higher negative ion count that has incredible health benefits like antimicrobial effect, mood-stabilizing impact, and increased levels of serotonin. According to WebMd's *Negative Ions Create Positive Vibes* article, the air circulating in the mountains and the beach contains tens of thousands of negative ions compared to the average home or office building that may measure anywhere from zero to a few hundred. It explains why we all migrate to such places on vacation. You can physically feel the benefits. When you change the environment, it changes the brain. Teams deliver more innovative ideas and see their team dynamics differently.

I started researching tree houses, glamping structures, dome homes, shipping container builds, and tiny houses. I could see different creative structures spread out across the property and a crown jewel of our renovated six-story tower revealing an epic 360-degree mountain view for miles. Just a dream or future reality? Who knows?

However, at the time, I still had a full-time job and extra time was not something I had a lot of. Then the unexpected happened. I got the call. We were selling our company to our competitor and as is normal for acquisitions, the existing executive team would exit post-transaction, including me. Even though I couldn't conceive of taking any time off from work just a few months before, now I was being presented with an opportunity to take a forced break. Exit stage left, so I thought.

In a surprising turn of events, there were many temptations to stay. Just when you think it is over, the universe loves to serve you temptation. I ended up temporarily extending my stay and taking over the acquiring company's marketing team due to their marketing executive resigning unexpectedly. Even though continuing to work would have been the easier decision for me, my soul was ready to explore something different. Given the executive team was in Los Angeles and I was in Atlanta, it just didn't align with my newfound desire to stay closer to home. The difficult choice was to give myself permission to take a break. I have been working since I was 14 years old. I had put an unbelievable amount of pressure on myself to climb, break through the proverbial glass ceiling, earn money, and live financially below my means. Taking a break scared the living daylights out of me. I had learned repetitively to trust my intuition and my intuition was screaming Soulbbatical with no work for at least a few months!

Note to Self

**Trust your intuition, that knowing inside your soul
that resonates in your bones.
It always knows the right answer for you.**

My intuition knew I needed some time to do a little soul searching. I was addicted to the busyness of my life. I had a feeling if I slowed down, I might discover a few things that could change my life for the better. I wanted to experience the simple joys of being. Shelley and several friends also challenged me on something that hit home and hit hard.

"So, you have modeled hard working, badassery, corporate guru, kick ass fun-loving adventure seeking Mom for your kids. How about modeling how radical self-care, joyful, relaxed Mom looks for them? Maybe show them it's okay to say no. It's okay to take a break. What would that look like?"

My answer: "The greatest gift I could give them."

I had truly never thought of it like that. It tugged at my heart. Kids are always observing and learning. I had always told them to take mental health days from school and was a maniac about them getting 8 to10 hours of sleep every night. I was telling them to go easy on themselves and as their mom I was saying the right things, but I was modeling a different behavior. They had observed me being hard on myself for their entire life. It was time for me to model something different.

Be careful what you wish for was my first thought as the last week of work approached. I was on my countdown to officially being unemployed. My feelings were all over the place. I had some relief and excitement, of course, but I also felt fear and sadness. I had to say goodbye to many I was close to, and if history taught me one thing, I knew most would not stay in touch. Most humans are just not good at staying in touch. It is not intentional. It is simply out of sight, out of mind.

I gave the job my all until the last day. It was part of my DNA work ethic. I could not slack off or stop working when I had committed to caring for the team to a certain date. It was important to me and my reputation to be loyal to the end. I like leaving any company on good terms. I had watched in disgust as individuals burned bridges, gave short notices, or took advantage of companies. It was disrespectful. I wasn't feeling good that week, but I chalked it up to the emotional aspect of leaving. I hadn't been sick in eight years. A quick trip to my naturopath confirmed I had strep throat. Interesting. I am about to take some time off and I suddenly get sick? The irony was not lost on me.

My team and my fellow executives gave me the greatest gift for my send off. They gave me gratitude, respect, and a journal full of letters. My team knew how much I loved letters. They had heard the stories of all the letters I had written to my kids and their friends over the years, so they all wrote me letters. What was in those letters meant more to me than any of the awards and accolades I had received in my career. I had done what I wanted to do in that chapter and the letters were affirmations for me. It is still one of my most treasured gifts. I have reread them many times.

As soon as I left my job, some incredible work opportunities came up because the job market was hot. I was tempted. Yet I noticed something I hadn't noticed before. All the job opportunities sounded the same. I couldn't get excited about any of them. I declined them all. I also started seeing the "busyness addiction" in everyone around me (including myself). It wasn't just that I was addicted to the busyness and constant challenges, I was addicted to a scheduled life. I listened and observed myself in my comfort zone of the respectable "crazy busy." I took a screenshot of my calendar that last week and saw the insanity. If I could just stop the busyness and unwind my patterns to see what was authentic for me and what was learned behavior or just mere habit. I didn't know how to not be busy.

Note to Self

**Busyness is just another form of addiction.
We all encourage it in each other.
The hardest thing I have ever done
was give myself permission to take a break.**

UNEMPLOYMENT: MY CHOSEN UNCOMFORTABLE NEW REALITY

The first day of my "official" unemployment was a Friday. I was free of a schedule for the first time in my life. It was surreal. I had strep throat, but my naturopath had given me her magic homeopathic drops for strep and the sore throat was already minimized. My husband and I took our boat out on the lake in the middle of the weekday and had a late lunch at a lakefront restaurant. Something we had never done together. Exactly what you might expect on the first day. Sunshine and no meetings. What is not to love, right? A lot. There was fear behind the scenes even on my first day. What was I going to do next? Why did I decline those really good job opportunities? What was I going to do to be productive? The stress, if we allow it, is equal to the stress of a busy work life. Isn't that fascinating?

I had decided not to put a timeframe on my unemployment. I just wanted to deprogram myself from the work/school schedule. I wanted to create a "to be" list, not a "to do" list. I wanted to do less "doing" and more "being." Sounds great, right? For someone else, but not for me. I lived by my to-do lists. I loved my to-do lists. Just "being" was so uncomfortable for me. I didn't know how to just be. I know how to set goals, work hard, and accomplish goals. I followed the Do, Have, Be model. That is all I knew. Now

I was attempting the BE model. It was like a foreign language to me. I wouldn't have lasted one week if it hadn't been for some key friends in my life that were reassessing their own lives at the same time.

I had to get comfortable with my discomfort. I had to get comfortable not being a high producer for the first time in my life. I had to give myself permission to rest and not feel shame about resting. I started noticing a different side to every conversation. When I would ask, "How are you?" Almost every person in my life would answer "Crazy busy." Just like I always answered. Every single person. For the first time, I only heard the "crazy" part. I think we all might be a little insane that we think being busy is a badge of honor. I consciously trained myself to answer differently, "I'm great, rested, healthy. I'm enjoying my life." Many didn't know how to respond. Giving myself permission to not be busy and not set goals was a whole new world. It was surprising how much courage it took to go against the norm. Being crazy busy alongside everyone else was so much easier for me. Then a comment from a podcast shocked me into a different mindset. I'm paraphrasing from memory here, but it was something like exhaustion blocks enlightenment and imagination. It keeps people trapped in a numb state so they can't think and connect the dots of things they want or don't want. Rest and prayer are as necessary as breath and water. Wow.

Note to Self

Stop wearing busy as a badge of honor.
Recognize the insanity of it.
Exhaustion blocks imagination.
Following the path less taken
requires so much more courage.

I wanted to focus on things I hadn't made time for previously like writing this book, mentoring young working women, home projects, studying different businesses and visiting nature retreats and glamping sites. I spent days unplugged which was in great contrast to my life as an executive. For years, my phone had been a constant flood of pings and rings with one emergency text or email after another. Hiking, silencing technology, and listening to the sounds of nature was filling my soul. Curvy gravel roads and no service areas were what I was craving more of. I took time to reconnect with old friends. I thought about whether I wanted to speed up or slow down for my next season. As always, I spent a lot of time with family and the relationships that were most important to me.

My relationship with my husband was top on the list. I was interested in a new kind of relationship with him. We were both good partners to each other. We were good at keeping busy and going through the motions of life together, but we weren't good at chilling with each other and more importantly receiving love from each other. We were a good match but there was a side of us that resisted having a truly healthy, great relationship. I wanted to change those dynamics. We both wanted to enjoy this next chapter of our lives together at a deeper level. I wanted our good relationship to be great. I just didn't know exactly what that meant yet.

My official second day of unemployment was interesting. I slept in, still wasn't feeling great. I laid low all day. My husband went to a Georgia Tech football game and by the time he got back I was in tremendous pain. My ear was throbbing. I had a fever. I got a warm wet washcloth and laid on my side to help relieve the ear pressure. The next thing I knew my eardrum burst and blood was coming out of my ear. The pain was intense. I asked my husband to check our insurance for an urgent care that was in the network. He came back with a look that said it all, "It says we aren't covered. We have no insurance coverage."

The reason this is so significant is that not having health insurance had been a fear of mine. I have no idea why. It is completely illogical. I had literally made multiple career decisions repeatedly so I could carry the insurance for our entire family as my husband was self-employed which limited our insurance options. Were there other options? Of course, there were, but sometimes our old beliefs block rational choices. There are many options for health insurance and the irony was we very rarely used health insurance. Knock on wood. Our primary care for the last twenty years was our naturopath and insurance didn't cover naturopathic care. Ridiculous and ludicrous, but true.

Here I was sick for the first time in eight years, unemployed, and being told we had no insurance. The universe was delivering all my greatest fears in one batch in the first 48 hours. I saw the humor in it. I also had enough self-awareness to know I was fine. The truth was we had health insurance, but Cobra takes a week or so to kick in. I also knew there was nothing urgent care could do for a ruptured eardrum. There was nothing to be fearful of, but our minds play tricks on us. We are human. I called my sister, who is a nurse, and she confirmed there was nothing to do but wait it out.

Within the first two weeks of my "blissful unemployed Soulbbatical," I had strep throat, a busted ear drum, a virus, poison ivy on my ass, and was bitten by a horse. One of my best friends reminded me it was God's way of saying sit your ass down and rest. I do believe our bodies tell us the truth about ourselves. Even when we appear very healthy on the outside, when we go through something significant or emotional, our bodies detox. I was detoxing. I had kept it together for a long time and I think my body was just letting it all out. Letting go. So, I accepted "being sick and tired" and I gave myself permission to rest.

This was one of many times in my life where I saw the emotional and physical connection. Our bodies are always talking to us. It's like we have this natural "check engine" light that comes on that says we need something. Our bodies start by whispering to us: tiredness, a mild headache, cough, allergies. We tend to pop a pill or grab a caffeinated drink and "push through" instead of listening to the whisper. Then the body raises its voice—anxiety attacks, migraines, eczema, insomnia, severe infections, gut issues, back problems. Some may start listening, but others ignore. As a last attempt the body yells—emergency room visit, back out for weeks, heart attack, stroke, disease. We are forced to listen. The insanity of it is that many people only listen for a short period even after the screams. They lay low for a week or two and then go back to their exact same lifestyle as if it never happened.

Even when we know better, we don't always do better. Something as simple as taking a break from electronics in the middle of the day can recharge your battery. Whenever my phone or laptop battery gets low, I take a break and try to go outside and put my bare feet in the grass. It recharges my own battery while I recharge my electronics. I also think better when I walk, so when I was in the office environment, I started instigating 'walk and talk' meetings as much as possible or just meeting outside versus in a conference room. Any little thing I could do to spend more time outside. At the simplest level, our bodies need sleep, oxygen, water, nutrition, movement, sunlight, and nature to function optimally. Listen to your body. What do I need to change?

Note to Self

My body always knows and sends me signals.
Whether I listen or not is up to me.
Even though we know better, we don't always do better.

———— ⦿ ————

THE GREAT RESIGNATION: A DIFFERENT VIEW OF THE CAUSE

What was I sick and tired of? My resignation happened to align with what was being called the "Great Resignation," a massive exit of corporate America. It was all over the news. Although I felt what was being said was opposite of what I was experiencing. Everyone was saying that women were resigning in larger numbers due to burnout and exhaustion. Much was talked about the COVID daycare situation and how it was harder on women than men. I remember feeling intense empathy for parents in general with young children during COVID. Juggling work and young kids with daycare was hard enough but COVID made it impossible. Given that household and childcare responsibilities typically fall more heavily on the female of the family, it made sense to me they were resigning. It was a sad fact I had been fighting most of my career. There is still very little equality in the home front even when both parents are working. We have come so far, yet not far enough.

I knew that was part of the Great Resignation story, but what I was experiencing was another part of the Great Resignation that wasn't being talked about as much. I had more time and more freedom to work than ever before. My kids were off at college. I also love to work with great people in great cultures. What I was witnessing in my network were executives in their late 40s or early 50s with and without kids, choosing to resign. Why? Why now?

I was getting calls from executives who had decided to take a break. They were from different size companies, and each had different roles, yet they were all describing the same issues. These were highly paid executives with successful track records. Two of us were CMOs, one was SVP of Business Development, one was SVP of Operations, and another was SVP of Human Resources. It wasn't burnout exhaustion in a physical sense. We all handled the jobs fine. It was exhaustion from toxic cultures, repetitive non-effective meetings, corporate amnesia, the denial of reality and the continued acceptance of incompetency. One described it as Groundhog Day every day. Different company, different teams, different meetings but the same old problems and same dysfunctional solutions, or worse, no solutions.

The "matrix" dysfunction of the corporate world was not fulfilling them. They loved many aspects of their work, but something was missing. The rules of the game were holding them back from using all their talents and being fully productive. This group of executives were describing situations that sounded all too familiar. When they spoke up in meetings, they weren't being heard. They were criticized for trying to drive too much change. Product was not delivering and in a cross functional meeting, the solution would be to create a new sales deck or marketing spin. One executive, out of utter frustration, said, "Here's an idea, how about the product team deliver what they said they were going to deliver. How is that for an option?" I laughed as I recalled saying that exact same thing before.

In many cases, these were "good" companies with positive employee cultures, but the lack of focus on the root problems and the accepted passive aggressive behavior was overpowering what we loved about working. One executive had a toxic founder that just flew off the handle and cursed out different people on different days and then acted like it never happened. It was "accepted" behavior. The lack of progress, lack of authentic conversations, and lack of efficiency was driving them insane. Many were expressing the desire to work for themselves and create purpose-filled businesses.

As I am writing this paragraph, Sheryl Sandberg, Chief Operating Officer (COO) of Meta, announced she was leaving her position. One of the top women in corporate America is voting and saying this isn't working for me anymore. She said this "moment for women" led her to make the decision to depart. "It's just not a job that leaves room for a lot of other stuff in your life. It is a really important moment for me to be able to do more." Sheri Salata, legendary producer for Oprah Winfrey, had chosen to leave a few years earlier. Shelley Paxton, former marketing executive for Harley Davidson, chose to leave. One of my best friends called me from her work parking lot saying, "I think I must quit right now." She just couldn't take "it" anymore. What was "it"? She quit without a plan. They were all consciously choosing to walk away. We all were seeking something more fulfilling. They were quitting because there was no purpose-filled, greater force of good, or they wanted to focus on a more holistic integrated life. There was a theme. Every single one of them, including myself, said I'm not done yet. In fact, I feel like my greatest season is the next one. We all wanted to work. That was not the issue. We just wanted a more fulfilling work culture.

Within my tiny corner of the world, the Great Resignation was not about burnout and pay. It is rarely about money. It is usually around lack of respect or work culture dynamics. Money is table stakes, meaning people expect to be paid at a fair market value for the job they are doing. If they are not paid their market value or if they are paid a lot less than their counterparts, then yes, they are dissatisfied and usually at some point will demand the company pay them fair market value or they will resign. Very rarely have I witnessed employees asking for more than market value. The equal pay fight for women is not asking for more than they deserve. It is simply asking companies to pay market value for a job regardless of whether the employee is a male or female, and not to favor males over females by offering them higher pay for the same job. When employees are paid fair market value which changes as market dynamics change, the majority say they would be satisfied financially speaking.

Also, I've noticed that if employees are working in a positive, non-toxic work environment, money very rarely comes up. When working in a toxic work environment, money always comes up. I will never forget one moment in my career, when this became so obvious. I was head of marketing for a company who acquired one of our competitors. The company we acquired had a very positive work culture. They were like a family to each other. The two founders were well respected, and the employees were not excited about the acquisition and very disappointed the founders were choosing to exit. The week following the transaction, we all met with many of the employees from the acquired company, welcoming them to our teams. There were many that expressed that they were paid significantly under market value. Many were asking for pay raises. In one conversation, I asked how long he had been at that salary. He replied, "Since my start date two years ago." So, he was satisfied with his salary for two years when he was working for the original founders, but one week under the acquiring company, the salary was unacceptable. Why? His answer was simple. The original founders respected him, and he was so grateful to work in such a fun environment with amazing people. He did not feel that way about the new company. There was no personal relationship with the "big" new company. Doesn't that say it all?

Here I was again hearing it in a different way. The Great Resignation was about work environments, not pay. They all expressed a simple desire, "I want to do great work with a great group of intelligent, equally contributing team members while serving a purpose-filled vision with forward growth progression."

What makes a negative work environment for employees? There is fear, the unknown, lack of progress or lack of respect to name a few. In one company in a twelve-month timeframe, I experienced three CEOs, three CTOs, two SVP of Sales, 2 SVPs of Customer Support and 2 CFOs. It was like a revolving door of executives. The direction for the company changed multiple times, exhausting and frustrating employees. It takes a lot of energy and usually a stall in progress for employees to adjust to new bosses or new team members. When any company has significant turnover for a long period of time, it is very demotivating to employees.

What I've observed repetitively is employees need a North Star that they can get behind. The greatest employee retention is solid vision, authenticity, progress, and respect. When a company or department is making progress, everyone seems to be happier. Progress is an adrenaline drug that gives energy to employees. Lack of progress is like a depressant that literally crushes employees' souls. Employees want to be seen, heard, and valued. Innate in most of us is a desire to be a part of an ethical community and something bigger than ourselves. If you can give employees that type of work environment, I guarantee you will have low employee turnover and higher productivity.

Note to Self

Employees desire clarity, passion, and respect.
They want a culture where they are heard and valued.
It is rarely about money. Progress is rewarding.

THE ENERGY WE BRING:
FINDING AUTHENTICITY

Energy is contagious—both the good and the bad energy. We all bring an energy with us. There have been people I literally had to stay away from in my life because their energy was just so negative—neighbors, bosses, coaches, coworkers, acquaintances. One boss would walk into a room, and it was like his mere presence sucked all the oxygen out of the room. Everyone else became quiet and intimidated. It didn't matter what day it was; it was just this negative, dark paranoid angry energy. In contrast, I have had bosses where they literally light up a room when they walk in. They bring that perfect combination of authenticity, confidence, and humbleness. They inspire everyone in the room to just do better by their mere presence. Pay attention to energy.

The greatest leaders I have witnessed are aware of their sphere of influence and the positive and negative behavior they choose. Other leaders just don't see the impact of their actions, or they simply don't care. If we don't have awareness, then we can't adjust.

I have found what is more important is what is at the center of our sphere of influence— how we lead ourselves. The act of becoming aware of our strengths and weaknesses and getting honest with ourselves. I noticed the slightest shifts could make a big difference in my daily energy. I shifted who I spent time with and who I didn't during this pause. It was amazing when I really started becoming more aware, how many people I realized were just so negative to be around. Then making more time for those that just make you feel good. Then the little things like something as simple as hiding certain individuals on my social feed and adding some fun-loving joyful people or funny accounts to follow can change everything. Choose wisely.

In the middle of this temporary time off, I conducted a few mentor sessions with younger working women in their 30s. One was struggling with finding what she called her authentic self and her management style. I shared with her how for me it changed over time and to not be so hard on herself. It is very common in our younger years to mirror the behavior of those we think have a better life than us. We tend to be more heavily influenced by others in our younger years. Everyone shifts and has that aha at a different age, but the process is just part of the journey. I explained how in the beginning of my career when I was younger, I took on many masculine leadership qualities because they were the only examples of leadership. As I got older, I realized my authentic leadership was a unique combination of feminine and masculine traits and I dropped many of the traits that no longer served me. I also dropped many of the old beliefs that I had inherited. My superpower was my unique blend. Her superpower is her unique blend.

We also discussed how common it is to chase the status quo dreams when we are younger. Many of us do things in the expected order—college, job, marriage, kids, house, etc. The status quo has a hundred unwritten rules to follow. We tend to follow rules like robots, never questioning what is right for us or what we truly want. Sometimes, we even follow other people's dreams until one day we wake up and realize it was our parent's dream or our friend's dream we were chasing. It was never our dream at all. It's not right or wrong, just more awareness.

We just took a moment to pause and rethink what felt right for her at this point in her life. What lights her on fire? What is important to her? How did she spend her free time? What was great about her job and what was nagging at her about her job? She was struggling with her work environment, thinking she needed to quit. She realized she was walking into the job with a negative attitude and with many wrong assumptions about her boss and the situation. What we discovered is that she just needed to shift how she interacted with her boss and her hours of work. There were many elements of the job she loved. Her perspective changed dramatically. She went from irritation to appreciation in a matter of minutes. It was interesting as her answers surprised her. That's the benefit of pausing and rethinking. She also added a little joy to her life. She started playing pickleball. Who would have thought three little shifts could change her weekly experience so dramatically.

Note to Self

**The energy we bring to the room is on us.
Shift your perspective of a situation and everything shifts.
Finding what is authentic for you is a journey.**

THE NEXT GENERATION:
DOING IT DIFFERENTLY

I look at the next generation and I am in awe of how they think and act compared to my own. The times they grew up in are very different. The access to information that they have through technology is completely different than the access my generation had. They also have so many more examples of diversity in leadership that I didn't have the privilege to see. They have grown up with more women and people of color in leadership roles. Albeit not nearly enough but far greater than I had. They see billionaire businesswomen as CEOs who created their own fortunes. Seeing yourself is essential to believing you can be something. It is why representation is so important in film, television, and leadership roles.

I hear so many criticize the next generation. I wonder if that is just a habit or if that is authentic. Every generation tends to criticize each other. My experience has been the opposite. I have so much respect for the wisdom of the generation before me and equal respect for the next generation, which I find very impressive. I recall the hours of conversation with my Cuban grandmother and all I learned from her even though our circumstances were completely different. The younger generation, those I managed and my family members, have taught me a different perspective and a different way of approaching life. There is something to be learned from each.

The next generation is changing the definition of work and career choices. My daughter did something I don't think I could have ever done at her age. She always dreamt of living out West, so she took a seasonal job at a five-star ranch in Montana after college versus the more common status quo job hunt using her college major. She is living another bucket list dream at 22. She lives rent free in one of the most beautiful places in our country. She is fly fishing, camping, snowboarding, cross country skiing, and rifle shooting after work. She is living where others vacation. One of her Montana friends has traveled all over the world. He has lived in Shanghai, London, Mexico, Alaska, Montana. He is a surfer, a pilot, a fisherman and so much more. He would decide what he wanted to learn or where he wanted to live for a period and then find a job to serve his passions. He had bought an airline ticket to a place he had never been without knowing where he would sleep once he got there. What a concept! For a planner like me that was inconceivable. Yet he had a lifetime of experience and cultural wisdom at the young age of 26. I admire their courage and how different they are from my 20-year-old self. I chose the "smart" route for a career in my 20s. I have no regrets for myself. It turned out well, but I admire how they are choosing to live their lives. It reiterated for me there are so many paths to choose.

My son chose to go to an academically-focused university and major in computer science. In his spare time, he has taught himself how to work on cars and participates in drift racing. He loves it. It is his passion. He has an old stick shift sports car with 140,000 miles on it. It's his first car. He, like his sister, had to pay for a third of the cost of their first car. He has used his own money to make numerous modifications to his car. He literally takes sections of his car apart and rebuilds it. He changes his own oil. He does things that most kids his age don't do. He exists in two completely different worlds, the computer science academic college world and the drift car racing world. He is happy. He is incorporating his dream of drifting cars into his post college plans. He jokingly says he is going to race cars for a living and his

Georgia Tech computer science degree is his backup plan. I have so much respect for how he has taught himself so many skills and his courage to race. Something I could never do and something that is difficult for me to watch him do, but it is his passion and his path, not mine.

Several of my nieces and nephews chose not to go to college. They have no debt. They are making a great living in construction and saving a ton of money. One niece is a ballerina, and one niece is on the football team. Others are going to college, and all have chosen very different majors. Some are working through college, some are not. Two nieces were D2 college athletes. One wants to do an international semester. Some are choosing to get married young and have kids right away. Others say they don't want to get married or have kids. They seem to know themselves a little better than my generation did at their age.

My point is that each of them are living their authentic lives. They are making the right choices for their desires and their beliefs. There is never one way for everyone. Respecting each other's differences and individual paths is essential to making this world a more interesting and peaceful place. Going against the status quo in many cases can be the smartest thing you ever do. It just must be authentic for you.

Note to Self

**Authenticity for each of us looks
different and that is okay.**

REDEFINING SUCCESS: GETTING RID OF THE "SHOULDAS"

During this Soulbbatical time, I was checking in with myself on what success means to me. It is a worthy exercise, redefining my definition of success with a broader view. There will still be career goals I want to accomplish but they are more around the type of leaders I want to work with and types of businesses, not necessarily job titles. The broader perspective is around how I want to feel, the life experiences and impact I want to have. Exploring places, cultures, nature, and wellness retreats are making the new definition. My mom and mother-in-law are two of the most important people in my life and they are turning 80 and 90 years old this year. I have consciously spent more time with them. How could I give back, I wondered. My time and my energy. Maya Angelou's quote was coming to mind over and over again, "People will forget what you said, people will forget what you did, but people will never forget how you made them feel."

I journaled a lot and even wrote about the type of people I wanted to work with in the future. The type of work environment and culture, focusing on what it felt like to collaborate with empowering individuals that were comfortable in their own skin. I journaled about different experiences I wanted to have with friends and family. It was around a feeling more than it was around a place or a job. It was a completely different type of thought process and description when you do it around how you want to feel versus what you want to do. Yet it was incredibly detailed.

I looked at all the roles I had chosen to play in life. There were ones I was playing consciously and unconsciously. I realized dropping a few made sense. When I chose to be more conscious of the roles that mattered to me, there was a certain magic present. Great things happen when we choose to focus our attention toward people and ideas. What I focused on improved—my health, relationships, mindset, or financial situation. How we choose to move and react to this crazy "brutiful" ordinarily amazing life is what we get out of it.

There is never one way, but a thousand ways to get to an end point. As my kids were starting to make their own money, they were asking me questions on spending, saving, and investing. It was all so confusing for them. I tried to remind them money is a necessary tool to function in this world. It's just not everything. You don't have to make a ton of money to be wealthy. You can save $100 a month starting at a young age, invest wisely and you will be a millionaire. You can live below your means and become wealthier than someone making twice as much money as you. Find a balance of spending, saving, and giving that feels right for you.

We know money can make things easier, but it does not make unhappy people happy. We talked about the happiest humans we had ever met were young orphan children in Zambia. They sang and danced every day. They had a blast playing soccer with a beat-up ball made of tape. Every day we were there they smiled. My kids were 6 and 9 years old when we went to Zambia to visit my brother and his family who were serving as missionaries in an orphanage at the time. My kids said two things about that trip. First, it was their favorite vacation ever. It was better than Disney World. Second, they noticed that orphan children in Africa were far happier than their friends back in the northern Atlanta suburbs who seemingly had everything. They were right about both.

Note to Self

**Happiness is an inside job.
Money is a necessary life tool.
Don't confuse the two.**

THE UNEXPECTED:
DON'T WAIT TO ENJOY LIFE

Another unexpected Soulbbatical surprise was dealing with grief. One of my college roommates had been diagnosed with terminal cancer earlier in the year. We had been friends for 32 years. She was "healthy" before the diagnosis. She was given the popular cancer protocol of chemo and radiation and told she had six months or less to live. Per her request, we planned a weekend with four of us, college friends, for November, a month into my time off. Her health took a severe turn for the worse the week before. We had to change our location. To say that weekend was special is the understatement of the century. We were fully present for each other, doing absolutely nothing for three days. Her physical limitations ended up being a gift of quality time together. We reminisced, laughed, cried, and even sat in silence. All four of us crawled in bed together and binge watched a comedy series. It was priceless. It was exactly what she wanted and a gift to the rest of us that we will never forget.

The reality check that someone my age was dying was heavy to comprehend. We shared the realization as we laid in that bed together that it could have been any of the four of us. Damned cancer was taking away someone I loved the most, again. It fueled my anger at our health system or sick system as I call it. Billions and billions of dollars donated to cancer research and still limited treatment options. Chemo and radiation thirty years later is still the "best" solution? Don't believe it. Hate it. There must be a better way. But for my dear sweet friend, it was not in her lifetime.

I was so grateful I had the benefit of time and flexibility to be fully present for a weekend with her. I've always felt I was racing against a clock, always pressed for time. I always fit it all in, but I was running from one thing to the next. Always feeling like I had limited flexibility as I had so many things I was juggling, from my kids' schedules to work schedules to friends and family events. I was always so proud of myself for "fitting" everything in and being so many places, but I always had the pressure of looming responsibilities around the corner. Being able to be flexible for others' schedules was so freeing. I knew it was temporary, so I soaked it all in.

Watching her handle this horrid disease and even worse life sentence was inspiring. She was present in a different way. She said to us, "I'm okay until I start thinking about the future. It's an odd feeling when I think next year I most likely will not be at our girls' weekend. That is when I get sad. But I am so thankful for this weekend." She was right.

Her new bucket list since her diagnosis was different than before. It was focused on spending time with those she loved. She made a trip to go see cousins, had several immediate family members come spend time with her, and our weekend. She wanted to make it through Thanksgiving and Christmas with her sisters, nieces, and nephews. She did and in January, we lost her. She was at peace, but all of us in her sphere of influence struggled. She is missed. The more you love someone the greater the grief. I always remind myself that it is a privilege to love someone deeply, but it hurts so much when you lose them.

One month later, a childhood friend, one of the most loving and finest humans I knew, lost his battle with cancer. He had outlived all medical predictions already, but his quality of life had deteriorated. He was my husband's age. At his funeral, it was inspiring to hear how his beautiful wife and family had handled the years prior to his passing. He possessed a selfless love, an undeniable faith, and a joyful attitude until his death.

How did he maintain a joyful spirit? Why does it seem like the good ones are taken too dang early? There are so many assholes in this world. Take the abusers, the narcissists, the murderers, the evil ones. Can't the good ones be spared? We need them.

Two friends, one my age and one my husband's age, were gone. I spent time alone thinking about the impact both had on me and all those they had touched in their lifetime. That is all we are left with at the end of our lives. The impact we have on each other.

Note to Self

**Time for my husband and me to live fully and joyfully.
Today is our only guarantee.**

THOSE WE LOVE MOST
TEACH US THE MOST
ABOUT OURSELVES

My husband and I discussed the obvious. Two individuals our exact ages. It could have been us. We both started talking and thinking a little differently. We went on a few vacations that we normally would have put off. We started some home renovations that our conservative financial nature might have passed on before. We were having that epiphany that life is short and none of us are guaranteed tomorrow. We didn't want to waste any time. We wanted to do what we wanted to do now, not later.

We shifted our mindset to just love and enjoy each other at a deeper level. Marriage is challenging. We had been together thirty years and like any long-term relationship there were many ups and downs. There are the simultaneous shared memories of great times and experiences with bad times and resentment. Witnessing death simply sharpens our perspective and gives us a sense of urgency to let go of all the baggage. We both just shifted a little and it made a world of difference. We became more open to receiving love. This was a surprise. We were both so fiercely independent and had created subconscious barriers to truly receiving and accepting love. I never thought that was an issue, but it was. I discovered that our needs change with each season of life. I had prided myself on being a different type of wife. I never wanted to fall into the stereotypical wife description. I made my own money. I took care of myself. I wasn't a big shopper. I didn't demand a date night. I didn't need romance. I could talk about business, finances, and sports with the boys. I was the least needy wife possible and proud of it.

In this season, I suddenly wanted the softer aspects in our relationship. I wanted to be taken care of for the first time in my life. I wanted more romance. I had to first understand for myself what it was I really wanted and needed. I had to get that straight in my head as this was new for me. Then I had to articulate it in a way to him that he could understand as I realized I was throwing a plot twist at him. Can I just tell you how hard those two steps were to figure out? It took me months. Lastly, I had to give him time to process as he didn't quite know what to do with this new version of me.

In every season of life, our needs and wants shift. Give yourself permission to change your mind, but you must give others around you the respect they are owed because you have changed the relationship. It takes communication, grace, and time. We shifted ever so slightly and it opened a new type of relationship. It wasn't as difficult as we had previously made it. Accepting love was harder than giving love. A fascinating discovery for both of us. I think many of us have a challenge in accepting love and self-sabotaging when we are on a path of greatness. Let the barriers down. Every one of us deserves to be loved. Let it happen.

Here's an analogy my spiritual advisor gave me. Two people have a relationship. For years, they walk around the same block. Around the second corner is a pothole. Every time they reach the pothole they fall in and then must climb their way out of it. One day, one of them says hey, there is a pothole right there, yet they both still fall in and must climb out again. Just the awareness that there is a pothole there didn't stop the habit of falling into the pothole. It continues over and over. Then one suggests they walk around the pothole to avoid it. One does yet the other one out of habit chooses to fall into the pothole. This time, the one that avoided the pothole provides the other one a hand up. The climbing out of the pothole was a little easier. This pattern repeats itself over and over until finally they both walk around the pothole. Things get easier. Then one suggests let's take a left instead of a right and see what is down this street. A whole new world opens. It's a view neither have ever seen. It's better. And sometimes, one says no, I like the going right only, and they go their separate ways. Each person in every relationship makes choices.

It can be in a friendship, sibling, spouse, mentor, or working relationship. You can repeat the same patterns, or one can change the game which inadvertently changes the whole relationship for the other person. Choose the path you want but respectfully let the other one choose the path they want. When you give those you love a plot twist, give them a little time to adapt.

Note to Self

**Let go of the struggle. Most of it is in your mind.
It doesn't have to be as hard as we make it.
Step around the potholes as much as possible.**

I have spent time with friends, and family, and watched my kids find their place in this world. They are both exactly where they are meant to be — opposite lives but both in their element. My son is finishing his college years, thinking about post-college decisions, and spending time exploring his car racing hobby. My daughter is loving and struggling with her life in Montana. My 50-year-old friends are following my daughter on social media, living vicariously through her. We are all secretly plotting to work as hourly employees for three months on a ranch out west for our "next season." Yet Lexie was doubting herself the whole time and stressed over her work. We humans are fascinating. We seem to always want whatever we don't have. What I wish for my kids is that they give themselves permission to change their minds, make shifts as needed in every season of their lives. I will always encourage them to constantly move toward the things that feed their soul and move away from the things that make them miserable. As that is what gets you closer and closer to your authentic life.

If I look back to when they were younger, both kids had made all the micro choices along the way heading straight toward their authentic selves. A few detours along the way, but they are both coming into their own. As a parent, I feel their unique paths seemed perfectly aligned with their personalities as toddlers. You can just see it as a parent. I don't want to sound too "Pollyanna" about raising kids, so let me recognize the stressful part of parenting. Like most parents I worried. I stressed about their health, drugs, alcohol, and safety. I worried about their social health, being accepted, or rejected by friend groups. I had to fight my desire to keep them bubble wrapped at home versus letting them go out into this scary world. When they experienced mental or physical pain, I could feel a visceral reaction in my body. I took them on adventurous almost dangerous experiences to build their "facing fear muscles" and at every single one, I was secretly scared to death they might get hurt. I went skydiving with my son and hiked Trolltunga in Norway with my daughter. We went whitewater rafting, rock climbing, skiing, and hiking where accidents were always possible. Then, they suddenly became braver than me. And in classic role reversals, they have both pushed me to do things with them that I was scared to death to do. Parenting challenges come full circle.

It was mentors, friends, sisters, and family that kept me in check over the years, reminding me my job as a parent is to teach them values, life skill sets, good decision-making, and how to be contributing, independent adults to society. My job was not to control or decide for them. They needed to fall, fail, and misstep. They needed to feel disappointment, pain, and difficulties. They needed to get hurt. I just needed to be there for them and love them through it all. Parenting is the hardest role most of us take on, yet it is by far the most rewarding.

Note to Self

**It's hard as a parent to let them fall.
It's rewarding as a parent when they
teach you what's best for them,
find their authentic path and
give you a few lessons about yourself.**

UNWINDING OLD HABITS AND
SEEING THINGS DIFFERENTLY

After an unexpected rough start, the Soulbbatical took a turn toward joy. I fumbled on many days without a schedule and clear goals. I felt a little lost because being productive was my love language. My level of productivity equaled my value, a strong belief that took many months to release. I settled into embracing the lack of schedule and enjoying it. I deprogrammed my brain from the weekly work schedule. I fell in love with Sundays again. There was no prep for the week required on Sundays. It changed everything. Sundays became my favorite day. I was also deprogramming myself from the comfort of having a work title, Chief Marketing Officer. I wanted to feel comfortable without a title, even if I chose to go back to the corporate world, which was highly likely. It was a real struggle at first, but I slowly got used to the idea of not "needing" the title. That was all it was about for me. I didn't want to need it, even if I had it again.

I spent a lot of time researching and studying all sorts of crazy next chapters. Giving myself the gift of freedom to explore things I had never explored before. I was trying things on and seeing how they felt. One day, I was researching online businesses and the next day how to become a mushroom farmer. I looked at buying a business and building a business. I was fascinated with the research. I looked at real estate investments and studied more stock investment theories. Having the time to research was incredible. Writing this book was a significant focus. It was thousands of hours of work and research, far harder than I had ever anticipated. I also defaulted on several occasions and replied to C-level job opportunities and consulting opportunities before I was ready. I had a few individuals get angry that I declined their opportunity. I noticed that certain relationships in life are conditional, especially in the work environment. When someone needs you, they call you. When you say yes and you help them, they adore you. When the opportunity is not good for you at the time and you say no, they might see it as rejection. They lose touch. Don't take it personally, just let it go. Remember people change in different seasons of their life and they may come back into your life, or they may not. Either is okay. Making the right decision for you at the time is more important.

The realization that two truths of one event could be true at the same time was a profound "Aha!" for me. My perspective of an event was my truth. It wasn't right and it wasn't wrong. It was my experience. However, my husband, my children, and my coworkers could have a completely different perspective of the same experience. They were not right or wrong. By mere nature, we all experience life differently. I read a quote that said, "we may be in the same storm, but we are rarely in the same boat experiencing the storm."

This analogy made so much sense to me. Some may be experiencing a storm from a military ship protected and secure while others are in an open raft getting hammered. Seeing a storm coming in, depending on which boat you are sitting in, can elicit a completely different response. For one person, it can mean a slight alteration in plans: stay home, don't venture out and enjoy a home-cooked meal. For others, it means getting hit with high-speed rain pellets fearful of loved ones slipping overboard.

In real life, I had seen the differences. When an hourly employee gets a flat tire on the way to work, his pay is docked, and he may be written up for being late or being a no show. He may not have a service to call to come get him, so it may take all day before someone can help him. The dock in pay may prevent him from making rent that month. He may not have the cash to fix the flat tire which can impact his life for weeks. His boss may be understanding or may tell him this is the first warning but if it happens again, you are fired.

When the CEO gets a flat tire, she calls a service, and it is taken care of in one hour. She calls her secretary to rearrange her meetings. She walks in and everyone is empathetic to her tardiness. They say things like, "I'm so sorry" or "What an inconvenience." She can afford a new tire. There is no other inconvenience or job impact than a 1 to 2 hour episode.

Everyone's circumstances are different. A global pandemic for someone who is immunocompromised may be the scariest time of their life. A global pandemic for someone who has a strong immune system, access to health practitioners, and a nice comfortable salary coming in may look more like a staycation, a break from an intense travel schedule. Coming back to the work office post COVID could be thrilling for one person and turn another person's life upside down. Same storm but very different experiences.

Note to Self

**Two truths can exist for one event.
Understand others may be experiencing
something very different from you.**

———— 💡 ————

WHAT I KNOW FOR SURE

I think my superpower is having the courage to trust my intuition, bring my authentic self to the table, and challenge the status quo, all with the intent for betterment. I gave myself permission to pause and rethink in every situation I came across that didn't feel right for me. I think when we all bring our whole selves with all our unique experiences, we can make a greater impact.

It feels like the world would be a much better place if we could all be a little more open minded and aware of others' circumstances and perspective. Being a little curious before the assumptions and judgment begin. Being a little more empathetic to the possible stressors others may be experiencing is being more human. We are all the sum of our total experiences. Who we are today will be different than who we are tomorrow.

Remember the boardroom moment at the beginning of the book? I even see it differently now. I see one 'bad egg' who wrongly influenced a few others. I have empathy for all involved who were just doing the best they could in a difficult situation. They saw things differently. I only saw things from my perspective. There was unfairness, no doubt. I learned from that experience, and I hope they learned from it as well. We are all doing the best we can with what we know at any given moment.

Many people have asked me what's next. For my next season, what I do isn't as important as how I do it and who I do it with. Like the best times of my career, I want to be surrounded by great people doing great things and helping each other make this world a little better even in the smallest way. I am still a bona fide *Hippie Capitalist*, building and growing profitable businesses is exhilarating for me. I like creating jobs and contributing to our economy. I just like to do it while respecting my fellow human beings, nature, my health, and my spirituality. In my office, you will find crystals, stones, and sage lying next to my laptop, spreadsheets, and presentations. I've just shifted my definition of success again. I'm still competitive and passionate about excelling at whatever I decide to do next. That part of me has not changed. I am simply more focused on fulfillment, doing work for a higher purpose and experiencing more "pure joy" moments during the day versus achieving goals. I've raised the bar. I don't expect to avoid problems or challenges, those will always be part of life. In fact, my greatest growth has come from challenging times. What is different is that I'm crystal clear on what I don't want, what I will not put up with anymore, and what I do want. I have more clarity on the things and people I say yes and no to. I don't waste time pleasing people. My intuition leads the way, and my ego takes a back seat.

This next season, like every next season, will be different than the one before. I'm a little wiser and I know myself far better than I knew my 20-year-old self, 30-year-old self, and 40-year-old self. What exactly it will be is still undefined, but I know it will be extraordinary, as I know and trust the author. In the meantime, I will continue to live more holistically. I've learned to breathe more deeply. When I eat, I savor every bite and when I laugh it encompasses my entire body. I continue to move toward the things that set my soul on fire, as that is when magical things start appearing in my life.

What I do know for sure is how each of us leads ourselves and those around us is a choice in business and in life. We all have a ripple effect on each other. There is always more to learn and always room to shift my perspective in each season. Life is meant to be enjoyed and shared.

Pause and *Rethink Everything* as often as you need to. Don't make it hard, just do it through the lens of awareness, authenticity, and accountability. Let simplicity, common sense, and curiosity lead a little more in your decision making. Find what works for you. It's your story, feel free to throw in a plot twist whenever you want.

Who Am I? I am.

What's My Story? It's still being written.

POST NOTE TO READER

RETHINK EVERYTHING—
THE BROADER PERSPECTIVE

In writing this book, I realized that the most valuable practice I had adopted in my 50-plus years on earth was the act of listening, pausing, and rethinking before just following the status quo. By not accepting everything that I was told that I should do or be, I found a better way for me. It created a habit of out-of-the-box thinking that better aligned my work and home lives with my heart and soul.

What I wish for my readers is that you give yourselves permission to rethink everything. Why? Because I think the world would be a better place for us all if we did. Sometimes we follow when we should be leading. Because our world is always changing, and sometimes the old rules don't make sense anymore. We are meant to evolve. We can learn something from every generation. We are meant to grow and do better, not repeat the same old mistakes. Is there a better way? Not always, but most likely.

Have you ever had that feeling when you hear something and every ounce of your being screams "that doesn't feel right." It's like your soul knows this doesn't work for you. This doesn't seem to be the smartest thing I could do or participate in. This feels like control for the sake of control. This feels like an unhealthy bias or hate. This feels like an unnecessary should. This—this just doesn't make sense. Sound familiar?

Rethink Everything goes beyond how we lead ourselves in business and in life. What if we were brave enough to rethink government, laws, education, companies, organizations, and even industries? Asking why can drive better solutions.

- *Why* is the "9 to 5 work week" that was created by Henry Ford for a manufacturing business model in the 1900s still the default schedule for today's digital world? Why do most people get in their car at the exact same time every day and cause a traffic jam?

- *Why* are there still only two political parties in the US in the 21st century, 200 years later when neither political party even comes close to representing so many that fall in the middle? Why does our political system require you to raise millions of dollars to run for office?

- *Why* do we teach US history so many times from kindergarten through high school, yet we don't teach entrepreneurship, finance, household management, career planning, mental health, meditation, goal setting, emotional intelligence, interview skills and tools to help the next generation manage life? Why does our school system still use a teaching style that forces kids to sit for 6 to 8 hours a day when we know it is horrible for their health to sit for that long? Why is our default teaching style still verbal lecture when most kids struggle to learn this way?

- *Why* is fighting for child care benefits in the corporate world a female issue? Isn't it a parental issue? Why aren't more working men demanding better childcare and taking paternity leave to help care for their children?

- *Why* do we prescribe drugs first instead of nutrition, nature, and exercise? Why does insurance only cover Western medicine and pharmaceutical prescriptions but not proven Eastern medicine techniques? Why don't medical doctors and naturopaths work together to help patients?

Is there a better way? What if we created "win-win" solutions like partnerships where both parties thrive? There are so many wise people and solutions that have already been developed but not widely implemented. Asking what if opens our mindset.

- *What if* we let private organizations support our educational system? What if we let successful technology entrepreneurs guest teach? Why not pay healthy restaurants to take over the horrific cafeteria food? Or, what if we took successful models, like the Ron Clark Academy and other organizations that have already figured it out and copied them?

- *What if* we built retirement homes and daycares next door to each other? Seniors are lonely and kids love to entertain seniors. Let's make it a trifecta and put a Humane Society in between a retirement home and a daycare, full of animals that need to be cared for and kids and seniors who might love to care for animals.

- *What if* we created wellness centers with affordable monthly subscription fees that health insurance covers? It would have medical doctors, naturopaths, chiropractors, acupuncturists, and many others that were there to keep you healthy and you'd go once a month for check-ins.

- *What if* we had prisoners produce something for the betterment of society that would make them feel useful and teach them a skill set at the same time? Could they produce a product that is sold and then used to pay for prisons to save tax dollars spent?

- *What if* we let middle school and high school students work for companies to experience what it is like to be an employee? We could make it part of the curriculum and give free labor to local small businesses. It could give them insight before they started choosing careers.

- *What if* we took our biggest problems and created a team of senior citizens and college kids who work together to solve the problems as the next reality show? The combination of wisdom and experience with youthful ideas and innovation could create radical solutions.

Win-win solutions require rethinking, redoing, and reimagining. They require change and most humans don't like change. There are benefits of the existing systems for a few and they will hold on for dear life before they will let you change it for the better.

Luckily, there are many who have the courage to lead change. Let's give credit to those wholly humans and amazing businesses who are being a force for good and rethinking everything. They are standing up to the status quo and they are doing amazing things.

- The CEO of Patagonia just left his billion-dollar company to Mother Earth instead of heirs. How is that for a creativity? Will he inspire others to think of new innovative options for leaving a legacy with their business and wealth?

- The large mega-corporations that are helping fund entrepreneurial start-ups that also create something of great value for the corporation. Dell for Entrepreneurs, Google for Entrepreneurs, HP for Entrepreneurs just to name a few programs that exist and are designed for a win-win solution.

- The entrepreneurs that created a tiny home community sharing resources like Acony Bell Tiny Home Village in western North Carolina. Also, the proven sustainable, nature-led community called Serenbe, outside of Atlanta, shows us there is a better way to create a "neighborhood." A community that is good for the Earth, good for people, and good for the soul.

- In low-income areas of Detroit, a brilliant human took vacant lots and transformed them into bee farms which created a natural ecosystem of health for the community. There are community gardens popping up across the United States.

- Acumen non-profit is investing in entrepreneurs to solve poverty issues around the world. They are not just giving money. They are not just helping them get started. They are helping them create a market ecosystem that will work for the long term.

- The many female and minority film and television stars, producers and writers who are creating content with stronger and more interesting female and minority storylines and characters. The Geena Davis Institute of Gender in Media research has reported an increase of female leads in family films from 24% (2007) to 48% (2019). Females are 50.5% of our population according to the U.S. Census Bureau. It is so refreshing to see movies and TV shows that are relatable for women and minorities and inching their way closer to representing our actual culture.

- Restaurants whose leftovers go to the homeless. Chef, humanitarian and founder of World Kitchen, Jose Andres, who I was honored to call a customer once, created a non-profit to feed those around the world who are suffering in the middle of disasters.

Let's do this. Let's rethink everything for ourselves as individuals, our families, our companies, and our world.

ACKNOWLEDGEMENTS

I must start with my family, all of them. Their love, support and encouragement propelled my life. When you can come home to a loving family, it gives you strength. I am forever indebted to each of them—my grandparents, parents, brother, sisters, husband, children, uncles, aunts, cousins, nieces, nephews, and my mother-in-law. My husband for always giving me the freedom and the room to be me, whatever that may mean in each season. Lexie and Jack, my kiddos, for being true to themselves and always teaching me more life lessons as they grow. My proudest and most rewarding role I have ever played is being your mother. You both amaze me every day. To my sisters, Teri and Jackie, for not just being sisters but being my best friends. You both are amazing working mothers and humans with phenomenal careers that inspired me.

To those who went on this year-long journey encouraging me when I wanted to throw this book in the trash. Susan Estroff, Teri Ullsperger, and Karin Fazzio, who were willing volunteer readers, and encouraged me daily through all the emotional ups and downs of writing this book. To all my volunteer readers who read the first drafts of the book that were not so good and gave me priceless constructive feedback: Laura Wilbanks, Amanda Barnes, Cam Lanier, Sydney Wilson, Kathy Jarvis, Jennifer Simmons, Lauren Schorr, and Jessica Harrison.

To my proofreaders, Nancy Harrison and Zollie Miles, who caught my mistakes before publication date. To my professional book coach, Patti Hall, who helped me in the beginning to outline the book and guided me through an endless number of cuts, edits and "rethinks." Your creative ideas and insights were invaluable. To Shelley Paxton, your book, coaching, and support guided me to a break I would have never given myself otherwise. To Jesse Sussman, coming in at the last leg and helping me get this book across the finish line. Your book publishing genius, encouragement, and recommendations made this book better.

To my dear friends and supporters that came in like you always do and supported me in the final chapter of getting this book across the line—Laura Anton, Dori Salisbury, Heather Heebner, Carmen Barretto, Paul Dodd, Craig Wood, and Carol Dunnigan. As if working with each of you wasn't enough of a gift, having you as friends is priceless.

To all my ballet friends and family at Columbia City Ballet Company of the 1980s, you were such a significant part of my life. The training, rehearsals, and performances were some of the greatest moments of my life. The discipline and the fun we had are memories to cherish.

To those early bosses and mentors that made such a positive impact on my career and my leadership style: Cheryl Walman, Kevin Toomey, Virginia McGrath, Mitch Bernatsky, Kevin Thigpen, Jay Galletly, Marvin Davis, Suzanne Beisner, and Cam Lanier. To all the CEOs, executive teams, investors, and boards, I've had the honor of serving, you taught me so many business and life lessons in how you chose to guide and lead.

To my friends that even with physical distance, you encourage me and support me with your mere presence and the many years of friendship: Sharon Bowman, Jacki Pyla, Jennifer Myers, Tina Altamura, Linda Austin, Alisa Arner, Deb Rigney, Angela McCurdy, and the late Dawn Keefner.

To all those I have had the privilege of working with in my career, your inspiration and teachings influenced who I am today. To the hundreds of incredible employees, I have had the honor to manage, I can't name you all, but know you taught me so much and you made me so proud. We built powerful dynamic teams that produced bottom line results. From talented creatives, digital geniuses, event executors, operational gurus to strategic communicators, you made leading joyful. I am forever grateful for all of it.

ABOUT THE AUTHOR

Kristi Turner is a C-level executive, thought leader, author, consultant, and mentor. She also happens to be mother of two, aunt to 14, sister, friend, daughter, and wife. By honoring every role and recognizing the relational benefits between them, her climb to Chief Marketing Officer in the heavily male-dominated private equity and venture capital funded high-growth technology industry is a lesson of courage, resilience, perseverance, and integrity.

Turner provides counsel to executive teams, investment firms and boards on brand, marketing, product design, customer operations, smart diversity, and employee culture. She has worked with some of the top retail, telecom and financial brands including Target, Walmart, Apple, T-Mobile, AT&T, American Express, and

Visa. Her favorite roles were guiding entrepreneurial companies from start-ups to multi-million high-growth companies. Turner has managed multiple companies through high growth, mergers, acquisitions, and crisis management. Turner has been interviewed and published in 50-plus publications and podcasts including *Forbes* and has coached C-suite executives for media and on-stage presentations. Turner is the recipient of a Lifetime Achievement Award for Top Women in Restaurant Technology as well as a Bronze Winner for promoting diversity at the 15th Annual Stevie Awards for Women in Business.

As a mentor, coach, and difference maker, Turner guides leaders and individuals through her Rethink Everything process in each unique season of life and business. Her radical simplicity and contagious energy inspire companies and individuals to adopt a different kind of leadership—one that delivers improved bottom-line results while making a difference in their community, and in their sphere of influence.

www.kristihturner.com

Made in the USA
Las Vegas, NV
19 April 2024

88875713R10156